Early Farming in Dalmatia

Early Farming in Dalmatia

Pokrovnik and Danilo Bitinj:
two Neolithic villages in southeast Europe

Andrew Moore, Marko Menđušić, Lawrence Brown,
Sue Colledge, Robert Giegengack, Thomas Higham,
Vladimir Hršak, Anthony Legge†, Drago Marguš,
Sarah McClure, Carol Palmer, Emil Podrug, Kelly Reed,
Jennifer Smith and Joško Zaninović

ARCHAEOPRESS PUBLISHING LTD
Summertown Pavilion
18-24 Middle Way
Summertown
Oxford OX2 7LG

www.archaeopress.com

ISBN 978-1-78969-158-0
ISBN 978-1-78969-159-7 (e-Pdf)

Cover image: Aerial view of the Danilo Valley, site of Danilo Bitinj in the middle distance, looking southeast (photo Šibenik Museum)

Printed in England by Oxuniprint, Oxford

This book is available direct from Archaeopress or from our website www.archaeopress.com

Contents

List of Figures and Tables

Figures

Tables

Preface

The Early Farming in Dalmatia Project began with an invitation. In March 2000 Andrew Moore was visiting the American College of Management and Technology in Dubrovnik, a satellite of his home institution, Rochester Institute of Technology in the USA. Colleagues at the College arranged for him to meet archaeologists in Split who would show him the main Neolithic sites in the region. That intriguing and informative excursion led to a meeting with Marko Menđušić who invited Andrew to join him in a collaborative project. This investigation would undertake a deeper exploration of key issues in the Neolithic and the development of farming in the central Adriatic. Two years later we began the project.

The project was conceived in the aftermath of the Homeland War which had ended a few years before. Archaeologists and other scientists in Croatia wanted to strengthen contacts with their western counterparts in the interests of building intellectual exchanges. For archaeology this meant bringing together the traditional expertise of Croatian archaeologists in the cultural record of their country with the new techniques and perspectives that their guests from abroad could deploy. There was indeed much to do, especially for prehistory. The great sites of the classical world in coastal Croatia, Split, Pula, Vis, Hvar, and others, were well known but the Neolithic sites were scarcely recognized. Maps of the later prehistory of Europe would leave the eastern shore of the Adriatic blank. This was despite the fact that substantial accounts of significant excavations carried out since the Second World War had been published in English and German.[1] This region formed the link between southeast Europe and the central and western Mediterranean. It should therefore have contained sites that could yield vital information for understanding the spread of agriculture and sedentary, village-based societies through the Mediterranean to southern Europe. Our project was intended to fill this void.

We have been joined by other archaeologists and scientists from Croatia, the USA, Britain and elsewhere who have recognized the potential importance of the region for later prehistory. Throughout, our collaborative research has proceeded in a spirit of generous cordiality. All participants have learned from each other: the team experts, skilled professional excavators, and students. Our results thus far demonstrate how productive this approach has been. Already, our project has generated an array of productive inquiries

---

[1] Korošec 1958-1959, 1964; Novak 1955.

leading to a series of publications and theses at the masters and doctoral levels.[2] It has also stimulated a new generation of international scholars to undertake research on the later prehistory of the region from a variety of innovative perspectives.

A major theme of our investigations has been to understand the human ecology of the earliest farming in Dalmatia and its later development. We have been especially interested in establishing the relationships between the history of the first agricultural villages as revealed by our excavations and the landscapes in which they were located. This context was an ever changing one, with human impact becoming increasingly significant as the Holocene advanced. We have also taken into account the influence of rising sea levels during the early Holocene, a more important element we now realize than we had thought at the outset. Much more needs to be done to expand our research with these perspectives in mind. That will be our task, and that of others, in the years to come.

Of the team that came together for the Early Farming in Dalmatia Project, one of its distinguished members is no longer with us. Tony Legge joined us in the field during several seasons, providing an immediate assessment of the significance of the faunal remains as they were recovered. His untimely death in 2013 was a great loss to us and to the world of archaeozoology.[3] Fortunately, he had completed his initial analysis of the animal bones from Pokrovnik and Danilo, and that research is included in this book.

This account represents a preliminary statement of our research thus far and our initial findings. We intend to pursue our inquiries further and to explore more fully the implications of the data we have recovered. We look forward to that task eagerly, stimulated by the rich insights that we have gained already.

Andrew Moore and Marko Menđušić
Autumn 2017

---

[2]   A partial list has been published in Menđušić and Moore 2013.
[3]   His friends and colleagues have compiled a book of essays in his honor, see Rowley-Conwy et al. 2017.

Acknowledgments

We express our warm thanks to the institutions that have sponsored our research. In Croatia this includes the Ministry of Culture in Zagreb and the Šibenik and Drniš museums, and in the USA Rochester Institute of Technology (RIT). The funding has come from grants from the National Geographic Society (NGS 7674-04), the National Science Foundation (NSF 0422195), RIT, and the Ministry of Culture in Croatia. The institutions we serve have provided support of various kinds, from travel grants to research facilities. The Research Laboratory for Archaeology and the History of Art, University of Oxford, has obtained nearly all the AMS determinations. Douglas Kennett (The Pennsylvania State University) has provided the others. The project has benefited from the hard work of many helpers from Danilo and Pokrovnik, and the efforts of students from several universities in Croatia, the USA and the United Kingdom. We offer special thanks to Stašo Forenbaher and Timothy Kaiser who read the final draft of this manuscript and offered helpful suggestions for improvement. We extend our deep appreciation to all those mentioned here, and to everyone else who has contributed to the successful continuation of the project.

Background to the research

The development of agriculture continues to be a vital subject of inquiry. It was, after all, the most significant transformation in human economy and society that has ever taken place, and it made possible most subsequent cultural developments. Moreover, the immediate impacts of this new economy on people, social organization, and the environment were profound. Most archaeologists and other scientists who have attempted to elucidate the processes by which this new way of life came into existence have concentrated their attention on the presumed centers of origin, of which the earliest was in western Asia. There are compelling reasons, however, for devoting equal attention to the initial spread of farming from these centers, for this process of diffusion can illuminate more clearly the immediate consequences of the transition to farming than the often lengthy formative phase in the original centers of development. Furthermore, such research can identify the processes of spread themselves, and so help us to address two of the most contentious issues in contemporary archaeology: how were these farming systems constituted, and what were the modes of transmission by which they traveled?[1]

Farming began in western Asia around 13,000 years ago, calibrated,[2] that is towards the end of the Late Glacial. By the mid Holocene it had dispersed through much of the temperate zone of the Old World and into North Africa. Of these episodes, the spread of farming around the Mediterranean and into Europe was as early as any. It is significant for its immediate impacts, certainly, but also because it provided the economic and social prerequisites for the development of the rich cultural complexity of later prehistoric and historic Europe. During the period of farming dispersal much of the Mediterranean Basin formed a single, distinct cultural region for the first time, as demonstrated by the ubiquity on coastal sites of the various kinds of impressed ware and of chipped obsidian tools from carefully selected sources. The rapidity of the spread of farming through the central and western Mediterranean and these indications of extended contact require attention and explanation.[3]

---

[1] Bellwood 2005: 2, 12; Colledge and Conolly 2007a; Fowler *et al.* 2015; Harris 1996: 7.
[2] Moore *et al.* 2000: 507; Zeder 2008: 11598.
[3] Isern *et al.* 2017

The Early Farming in Dalmatia Project has been designed to investigate the spread of farming to the Adriatic and, in particular, the Dalmatian coast. The Adriatic Basin is important because it forms the bridge between southeast Europe and the lands to the west. The project is intended to serve as a case study of the broader dispersal of this new way of life through the central and western Mediterranean. We are attempting to answer a number of questions, of which the most important may be stated at the outset. First, when did farming reach Dalmatia? Second, how did it get there? Third, what was the nature of this economy? Fourth, what were the climate and landscape like at the time of arrival and how did they influence the development of agriculture? Next, what, if any, were the responses of the local Mesolithic population to the coming of farming? Sixth, what impact did farming have on the region, and what sorts of communities developed there through the Neolithic? We have had considerable success in establishing the nature of the farming economy, the date of its inception, and the character of these early farming communities. Their interactions with the landscape will, however, require substantial further research as the project proceeds.

Our methodological approach is distinctive. From the outset, the project has been designed as a multidisciplinary exercise in ecological research, with significant contributions from geologists, botanists, and physical scientists, as well as from archaeobotanists and archaeozoologists. We have used a comprehensive recovery strategy in our excavations, and wherever possible have deployed up-to-date technologies to aid our investigations. To deepen our understanding of agricultural practices in the Neolithic we have conducted inquiries into traditional farming among local farmers. The inspiration for the project arose from a compelling need to address important issues of concern to archaeology, but the scope is far wider than this. The project is a new departure in approaches to archaeological research in Croatia,[4] and its configuration is unusual among parallel investigations around the Mediterranean and in southern Europe. It represents an expansion of perspectives developed by several of us in research on the early inception of farming in the Euphrates Valley in Syria.[5]

We have known from the time of Childe[6] that farming spread from the Middle East to Europe along two routes, by land up the Danube into central Europe, and by sea around the Mediterranean to the shores of southern Europe. The natures of the agricultural systems that were dispersed and the modes of their transmission have been topics of fierce and continuing debate. Several recently published compendiums provide succinct summaries of these varying points of view.[7] Archaeologists and others who investigate these matters in the Mediterranean Basin and beyond have offered a variety of interpretations of what actually happened. At one extreme are those who have argued that the development of farming in Europe owed very little either to agricultural systems developed elsewhere or to immigrant farmers,[8] views that are heard less often now.[9] Others, while allowing that

[4]   Davison et al. 2017; Moore and Menđušić 2004; Menđušić and Moore 2013.
[5]   Moore et al. 2000.
[6]   Childe 1957: chapters VI and XIII.
[7]   Ammerman and Biagi 2003; Cummings et al. 2014; Fowler et al. 2015; Price 2000.
[8]   Donahue 1992; Whittle 1996: 360-361.
[9]   Note, however, Kyparissi-Apostolika 2002, 2007; Marijanović, 2009: 246; and Séfériadès 2002.

the domesticates themselves, both plants and animals, originated in western Asia, consider the spread of farming to have been a patchy affair that depended in part on the responses of indigenous Mesolithic hunter-gatherers to the appearance of this new way of life.[10] They argue, further, that very little of a farming economy was transmitted in the early stages, and that hunting and gathering remained important well into the Neolithic.[11] For the Mediterranean, at least, there is a solidifying body of opinion, based on the substantial accumulation of new data, which supports the view that a mature, subsistence farming system, embracing a suite of domestic crops and animals, was carried along the coast by migrating farmers who established their villages in places favorable for arable agriculture.[12]

That it is possible to advance such varying interpretations is in part because in regions as extensive and environmentally diverse as Mediterranean, central, and northern Europe it would be reasonable to expect that the spread of farming and the interactions between farmers and indigenous foragers would have been complex processes. It is also because many excavators of Neolithic sites have used traditional methods that have not been directed towards recovery of plant and animal remains. One result has been that in the Mediterranean archaeologists have often taken the arrival of pottery as a proxy for the dissemination of farming.[13] This co-occurrence, of the first pottery and the initial stages of farming, on Neolithic sites does seem to reflect what happened, but it tells us nothing about the nature of these early agricultural systems, nor how they were adapted to the varying landscapes of the Mediterranean Basin.

Archaeologists working within Croatia have expressed a similar diversity of views on the inception of farming as their colleagues elsewhere in Europe. The pioneering prehistorian Grga Novak who excavated the key site of Grapčeva spilja on Hvar concluded that the successive Neolithic cultures he documented there were derived from the eastern Mediterranean through maritime contact.[14] That view has largely been superseded by a recognition that the pottery, at least, had its own local history of development. Croatian archaeologists who conduct research on Neolithic sites agree that the plant and animal domesticates originated in western Asia.[15] Nonetheless, some would argue that farming was adopted by the indigenous Mesolithic population, and that hunting and gathering remained an important element of the economy well into the Neolithic.[16] They consider that farming had relatively little impact until later times. Indeed, it is commonly asserted that the natural environment, and the vegetation in particular, remained undisturbed by farming activities until the Bronze Age or even later.[17] These views have been challenged by others who argue that farming took hold quite early in the Neolithic.[18]

---

[10] Zvelebil and Lillie 2000.
[11] Price 2003: 280-281.
[12] Forenbaher and Miracle 2014; Isern *et al.* 2017; Kaiser and Forenbaher 2016a: 159-160; Zeder 2008; Zilhão 2003.
[13] Barnett 2000: 96.
[14] Novak 1955: 328–329.
[15] Forenbaher and Kaiser 2005: 16.
[16] For example Bass 2008: 258; Batović 1968: 11; Marijanović 2000: 212, 231; Marijanović 2009: 249-251.
[17] Šoštarić 2005: 384-385.
[18] Chapman *et al.* 1996: 259; Forenbaher 1999: 524.

Relatively little research has been carried out on the problem of the development of farming in the Adriatic Basin, so there are simply insufficient data available to address the key issues effectively. Adequate samples of plant remains and animal bones do not exist, and until recently the known radiocarbon dates were too few for precise chronological determinations. This difficulty was compounded by the fact that many of the dates were obtained from charcoal using conventional techniques, rather than samples from short-lived species of plants and animals dated by accelerator mass spectrometry (AMS).

The Neolithic in the Adriatic Basin was preceded by a Mesolithic phase that has yet to be well defined. Few Mesolithic sites have been identified in Dalmatia, making it difficult to understand the nature of human activity there preceding the arrival of agriculture. Some, perhaps many, sites will have been drowned by the continued rise in sea level during the early Holocene,[19] but this is insufficient an explanation for the dearth of known sites. Concentrations of Mesolithic open and cave sites have been discovered in Istria and the adjacent offshore islands in recent, carefully-targeted, surveys.[20] In one of these sites, Pupićina Cave, meticulous excavations have revealed early Mesolithic deposits.[21] The Mesolithic inhabitants of another well-known site, Vela spila on the island of Korčula, derived a good deal of their sustenance from fishing, judging by the abundant bones of mackerel, tuna, swordfish and other species found in the deposits.[22] These discoveries notwithstanding, the record of Mesolithic occupation in Dalmatia is sparse.

In central and southern Europe there appears to have been a significant gap between the latest dates for Mesolithic occupation and the earliest for Neolithic farming settlements.[23] This trend is particularly marked in Mediterranean Europe, including the Adriatic, where the two episodes appear to have been separated by many centuries.[24] The hiatus has been identified at Pupićina Cave for example.[25] This may partly explain the current minimal evidence for Mesolithic occupation in Dalmatia immediately prior to the beginning of the Neolithic and the first agricultural settlements.

---

[19] Moore 2014.
[20] Komšo 2006.
[21] Miracle and Forenbaher 2006: 456.
[22] Čečuk and Radić 2005: 61-62; Rainsford et al. 2014.
[23] Gkiasta et al. 2003: 56, 59.
[24] Biagi and Spataro 1999-2000.
[25] Miracle and Forenbaher 2006: 455-458.

Inception of the project

In March 2000, during a visit to Danilo Bitinj and Pokrovnik, Menđušić, then Senior Curator for Prehistory in the City Museum of Šibenik, invited Moore to undertake an archaeological project with him that would focus on the Neolithic. Two years elapsed before Moore could take up this generous invitation. Then, in 2002 we began to design and implement a longer-term collaborative research project that would renew investigation of the Neolithic in Dalmatia with a special emphasis on improving our understanding of the development of farming there. We visited Neolithic sites and museums with collections of Neolithic material from Istria in the north to Split in the south. While highly informative, this exercise soon indicated to us that the few sites with the potential to answer questions of interest to us lay in northern Dalmatia. It is there that we have concentrated our efforts.

Our collaboration was intended to combine the rich archaeological knowledge of our Croatian colleagues, especially for the later prehistory of Dalmatia, with the ecological perspective espoused by the American and other international participants.[26] Our Croatian colleagues possessed a profound understanding of the natural history of the region that has been of special value to the project. A further aim was to deploy a broad array of advanced technological investigative techniques to address the questions we wished to resolve. Among these were ground penetrating radar (GPR) for site survey, and AMS dating. The project is sponsored by the Šibenik Museum, Drniš Museum, and Ministry of Culture in Croatia and Rochester Institute of Technology (RIT) in the USA. Numerous other bodies in Croatia, the USA and other countries have since joined in supporting the research (see the Acknowledgments).

South of the Istrian Peninsula the Adriatic coast of Croatia consists of an intermittent coastal strip backed by the formidable massif of the Dinaric Alps. For most of their 400 km length the front range of these karst mountains falls straight into the sea. In northern Dalmatia, from Zadar to Split, there lies a 40 km-wide zone of narrow valleys and hills between the Adriatic and the looming presence of Mount Dinara itself on the eastern horizon. The floors of these valleys contain rich soils that are heavily cultivated today. Offshore, a chain of over 1,000 islands and islets runs parallel to the entire length of the coast and extends half way across the Adriatic. Small, outlying islands provide intervisible landfalls as far as

---

[26] Menđušić and Moore 2013.

the Italian coast. Dalmatia is thus open to the sea but separated from inland Europe by the Dinaric range, and this circumstance has affected the cultural development of the region far back in time.[27]

Much of the research on the later prehistory of Dalmatia in recent decades has taken place on the islands. There have been extensive surveys of Hvar, Brač, and a number of smaller islands.[28] An important excavation of the deeply stratified deposits at Vela spila on Korčula[29] and investigations of a number of sites on outlying islands[30] give an indication of the scope of this research. On the islands and on the mainland, archaeologists investigating the later prehistory of the eastern Adriatic have preferred to excavate caves and rockshelters.[31] This is because these sites provide evidence of long-term cultural changes. However, they suffer from systemic bioturbation by humans and wild fauna, causing mixing of the deposits. Many of the caves and shelters are located in the karstic hills and mountains in places unsuitable for farming, though they have been used on occasion by pastoralists. Consequently, they have little to tell us about the development of agriculture in the region. In contrast, we decided to investigate open village sites in areas that are heavily farmed today because they were more likely to yield the kinds of evidence we sought. The most promising sites were in the fertile valleys of northern Dalmatia, particularly those in the Šibenik region.

Selection of Danilo and Pokrovnik

We decided at the outset that the most efficient way to proceed would be to choose sites that had been occupied in more than one phase of the Neolithic because we wished to ascertain how economy and culture had changed through time. Furthermore, the sites selected should offer good preservation of organic material, mainly animal bones and charred plant remains, as well as artifacts. This was essential if we were to recover adequate samples to address questions of agricultural development. It followed that such sites would have been excavated before.

These criteria were sufficiently stringent that our choice proved to be limited. Happily two sites, Danilo Bitinj and Pokrovnik, met our needs (Figure 1). Danilo Bitinj[32] was located 8 km inland from the present-day coastline, at the center of a 6 km long valley (Figure 2). This valley is heavily cultivated today in a mixed farming regime that includes cereals, vines, fruit trees, olives and hay with some sheep, cattle, pigs and poultry. Danilo Bitinj, or Danilo for short, was an extensive settlement and the typesite for the Middle Neolithic in Dalmatia (Figure 3). Excavations there by Korošec in the 1950s had yielded animal bones, marine shells and impressions of cereal grains in daub.[33] Thus, the site contained organic material that would aid in economic analysis. Pokrovnik was in the next valley inland, some 18 km from the coast. It lay in an embayment at the foot of a range of hills; to the west the land

---

[27] Violich, F. 1998: 76-77.
[28] Gaffney and Kirigin (eds.) 2006; Gaffney *et al.* 1997; Stančič *et al.* 1999.
[29] Čečuk and Radić 2005.
[30] Forenbaher 1999, (ed.) 2009, 2018; Forenbaher and Kaiser 2005.
[31] Kaiser and Forenbaher 2012, 2016b; Miracle and Forenbaher (eds.) 2006; Novak 1955; Čečuk and Radić 2005; Marijanović 2005.
[32] Bitinj is the name given to the well that is a conspicuous feature in the center of the Danilo Valley.
[33] Hopf 1964.

opened onto an undulating plain with another ridge on the horizon (Figure 4). The open ground in front of the site was cultivated as at Danilo while the hills behind were used for rough grazing. Pokrovnik was less extensive than Danilo but was known to contain relatively deep deposits of the Early and Middle Neolithic with preservation of organic material.[34] It thus complemented the sequence from Danilo. As the two sites were in different locations, it would be possible to compare their cultural and economic sequences to see if this had had any effect on the way of life of their inhabitants. We conducted a GPR survey of Danilo in 2003 and excavated there in 2004 and 2005. Our research at Pokrovnik began with a GPR survey in 2004, followed by excavations in 2006. Concurrently, our colleagues in geology and botany began their investigations of the geomorphology and vegetation of the region, research that is continuing. Following the conclusion of the excavations, we have begun an intensive study of the artifacts from both sites. Some initial results of those analyses are reported here.

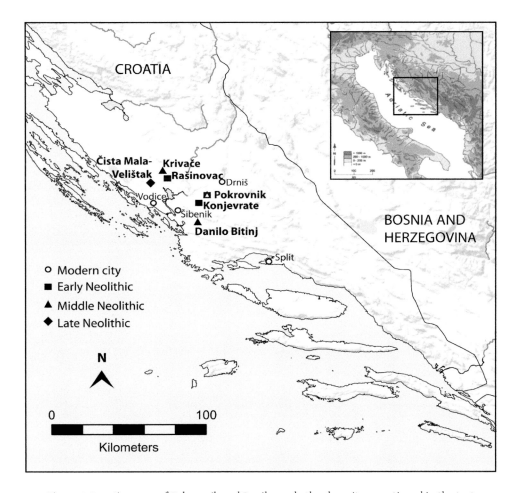

Figure 1. Location map of Pokrovnik and Danilo, and other key sites mentioned in the text.

---

[34] Menđušić 1998: 52-55.

Figure 2. Aerial view of the Danilo Valley looking west. The site of Danilo Bitinj is in the middle distance; the Adriatic Sea is visible on the horizon (photo Šibenik Museum).

Figure 3. Aerial view of the site of Danilo Bitinj, looking southeast (photo Šibenik Museum).

Figure 4. View of the site of Pokrovnik from the northeast. The Pećina spring is in the grove of hackberry trees to the left of center.

History of research at Danilo Bitinj and Pokrovnik

The area surrounding the spring and well named Bitinj in the Danilo Valley was known to be a prehistoric site long before the first excavation there, due to the numerous surface finds uncovered by local villagers in their vineyards. In the summer of 1951 Professor Duje Rendić Miočević, the excavator of the nearby Roman villa, placed a small test trench in the vicinity of the Bitinj well in order to examine the precise location and character of the site. The trench gave positive results with a large quantity of finds, especially pottery fragments of an unknown prehistoric culture.[35] It was clear that this site merited more attention.

Danilo Bitinj was excavated by Professor Josip Korošec in the summers of 1953 and 1955, under the aegis of the Yugoslavian Academy of Science and Art and in collaboration with Ivan Marović, Curator of Prehistory at the Archaeological Museum of Split, and Frano Dujmović, Director of the City Museum of Šibenik. It was one of the first excavations of a Neolithic site in Dalmatia and perhaps the most extensive excavation of a Neolithic village in the Adriatic region to date. Korošec opened three large trenches on three strip fields, and a set of smaller test trenches in neighboring land parcels. A total area of around 2,500 m2 was explored and part of a much larger settlement revealed. Between humus and sterile subsoil, the average thickness of the cultural layers ranged from 0.60-1.00 m. Korošec found no traces of dwellings except isolated fragments of burned daub wall with wattle impressions. He identified a simplified vertical stratigraphy, which should be attributed to the pioneer character of his excavation methods. The only structures revealed were circular or irregularly shaped pits dug into the subsoil. But finds were numerous: besides stone, flint and bone artifacts the most intriguing was the pottery assemblage. This included vessel shapes and techniques of ornamentation that differed from other eastern Adriatic Neolithic cultures known at that time. Korošec named this new assemblage the Danilo culture, and placed it in the Middle Neolithic.[36]

---

[35] Korošec 1952.
[36] Korošec 1958-1959.

In the several decades that have followed, intensive research into the Neolithic, both on open area and in cave sites, has shown that the Danilo culture and its local variants covered most of the eastern Adriatic coast and its hinterland.[37]

The next excavation at Danilo was undertaken in 1992 by Menđušić. Part of the site was endangered by construction work surrounding the resurfacing of the cross-valley road. In a salvage excavation Menđušić opened two trenches measuring around 60 m² in area. This time, irregularly preserved traces of a floor of a dwelling, a hearth and many fragments of house daub were found, besides a large quantity of pottery and other small finds.[38]

The Neolithic site in the village of Pokrovnik was discovered in 1979 during tractor plowing in the vineyards, close to the Pećina spring at the foot of the hill topped by the church of Sveti Mihovil (Saint Michael) (Figure 4). Immediately after, in the summer of 1979, Professor Zdenko Brusić, then Curator of Prehistory in the City Museum of Šibenik, conducted a partial rescue excavation. He opened seven trenches of varying dimensions on three strip fields. In total, he explored an area of 114 m². As the depth of the trenches varied from 0.45 to 2.05 m from the subsoil to the modern land surface, so did the thickness of the Early and Middle Neolithic layers; in the deepest trenches these were correspondingly substantial, that is about 1 m each. Besides a large quantity of small finds, Brusić also found traces of hearths and drystone walls. Results of the pottery analyses revealed that Pokrovnik contained substantial deposits of Early Neolithic ("*Impresso*" or Impressed Ware culture) and Middle Neolithic (Danilo culture) and, based on a small number of pottery fragments in the surface layers, a Late Neolithic (Hvar culture) phase also.[39]

There were no further excavations at the site until we began work in 2006.

---

[37] Batović 1979: 524-526.
[38] Menđušić 1993, 1998.
[39] Brusić 1979; Brusić 2008; Menđušić 1995: 18-23; Menđušić 1998: 52-54; Menđušić 2005: 90-92.

Excavations at Danilo Bitinj and Pokrovnik
2003-2006

Danilo and Pokrovnik were heavily cultivated and there were no visible archaeological structures on the surface. Consequently, we decided to begin by conducting a GPR survey of part of each site and to base the decision on where to place the excavation trenches on its results. There were other constraints on the location of the trenches, principally the availability of fallow land within the many strip fields into which the surface of each site had been divided.

Danilo 2003-2005

The site lies at the lowest point of the Danilo Valley and much of it becomes heavily waterlogged in wet winters. Thus, most of the surface of the site is covered with hay meadows. The rest is planted with vines or used for arable crops (Figure 5). The surface has been heavily eroded, so an unknown amount of the prehistoric settlement has disappeared. A seasonal stream, the Dabar, runs along the south edge. This stream has cut through the hills to the next valley, Donje Polje, and thence to the sea. The Dabar thus provides the main surface drainage out of the Danilo Valley.

There was a scattering of pieces of daub, marine shells and artifacts across the surface of the site. The soil was a distinctive grey color in contrast to the brown and red soils of *terra rossa* type characteristic of the Danilo Valley. Recent disturbance of the surface through construction activities provided further indications of the extent of the prehistoric occupation. Taking all this information together, we estimate that the Neolithic site covered over 9 ha.

We selected five strip fields in the center of the site for survey using GPR, beginning in the March 2003 season and continuing in the summer of 2004.[40] These fields were located on both sides of the road that bisects the site. In all, the survey covered 8,900 m². To complete the GPR investigations, we ran a transect 370 m long across the site from east to west.

---

[40] The survey was carried out by students under the direction of Professor Larry Brown of Cornell University (See Haenlein 2003). In 2003 the students were Joel Haenlein and Stephen Romaniello, and in 2004 Kristen Romano. Ida Koncani from the University of Zadar, and now at the Istrian Archaeological Museum in Pula, assisted in 2003.

Figure 5. The site of Danilo from the northeast. The Dabar stream runs along the far side of the site beside the valley road.

The results were unequivocal: nearly all the transects revealed evidence of sub-surface anomalies that were likely the remains of features created by ancient inhabitants of the site. To validate this information, in the initial 2003 season we dug a small trench 1 by 2 m in area in Field 1 to test a strong anomaly. The excavation revealed a hearth and a length of stone wall, thus corroborating the evidence from the GPR survey. The finds consisted of potsherds, flint, obsidian, charcoal, animal bones, and cockle shells. This suggested that in subsequent excavations we should be able to recover significant samples of bones and charred plant remains to ascertain the economy of the ancient inhabitants.

Given the extent of the site and the indications of widespread as well as dense occupation, we decided to space our trenches out across the fields available to us in order to determine something of the layout of the prehistoric settlement and any differences in use from one area to another. We took care also to locate them at some distance from the very large trenches excavated by Korošec. In all we excavated five trenches, A to E, two (A, B) in Field 1, a third (C) in Field 2, the fourth (D) in Field 3, and a fifth (E) adjacent to the trench beside the road that Menđušić had dug in 1992 (Figure 6). The latter was sited to explore further the evidence he had found for clay-walled houses in this area.

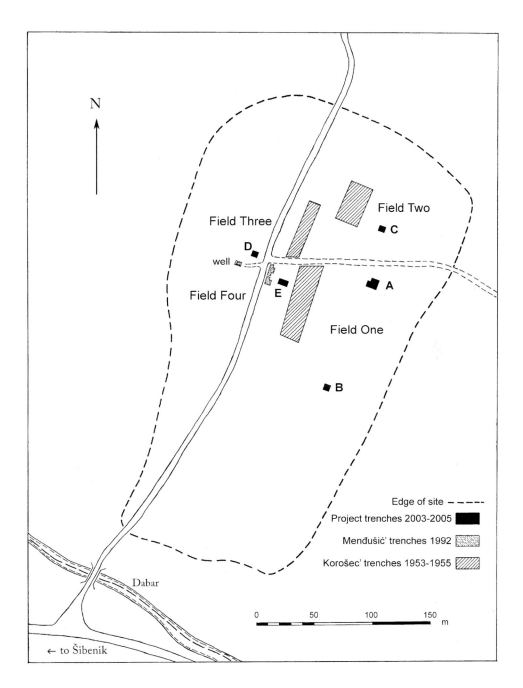

Figure 6. Plan of the site of Danilo showing the locations of the trenches we excavated. The locations of the trenches dug by Korošec (1953, 1955) and Menđušić (1992) are also indicated.

Methods of excavation

Following the test excavation in 2003, we planned to excavate one trench in 2004 and then to dig more extensively in the 2005 season. This measured approach proved to be appropriate as it enabled us to adjust our methods to suit the local conditions. The trenches were excavated stratigraphically down to the natural subsoil using hand tools. We used a standard paper-based recording system in the field,[41] supplemented by an extensive photographic record compiled with both film and digital cameras. All materials recovered were recorded in a computer database for subsequent analysis.

In order to ensure as nearly as possible complete recovery of artifacts, bones, shells, and charred plant remains, we had planned to water sieve all the excavated deposits using a flotation machine developed at RIT. In the 2004 season this soon proved to be impracticable because the soil at Danilo was a heavy, dense clay that clogged the machine. Furthermore, the soil also contained many stones that hindered progress. So we altered our strategy to dry-sieve all the soil first using sieves with a 8 mm mesh and then to pass as much of the soil as possible through the flotation machine. This was equipped with a 250 micron sieve to retrieve the plant remains. The modified approach yielded a sample of plant remains and ensured almost complete recovery of artifacts and bones. In the 2005 season, on the advice of Sue Colledge, archaeobotanist, who joined us in the field, we adjusted our strategy once more. This was because the plant remains were extremely fragile and so liable to be damaged in the dry sieving prior to flotation. Colledge recommended that we take substantial samples of soil from each level excavated that contained plant remains and pass these through the two flotation machines we deployed in 2005, sorting the residue later to recover the artifacts. The rest of the soil could be sieved in the usual manner. This hybrid system yielded as large a sample of plant remains as was practicable and near complete recovery of everything else with less damage overall. The residues from the flotation were hand sorted to extract all items of interest. Normally, this would have included very small bones as well as artifacts. We found, however, that little such material was present in the residues from Danilo. We attributed this to long-term expansion and contraction of the clay soils that had apparently destroyed almost all such minute fragile remains.

We used a similar recovery system at Pokrovnik in 2006. By this time most of the issues had been resolved and excellent results were achieved. The soil at Pokrovnik proved to be less inimical to preservation of artifacts and organic remains.

The excavations at Danilo in 2004 and 2005

In 2004 we excavated one trench, Trench A, five by five meters in size, in Field 1, adjacent to the small sounding dug in 2003. The location was determined by a concentration of anomalies revealed by the GPR survey. Our aim was to begin to define the stratigraphic sequence of occupation at Danilo and also the main structures and other features of the Neolithic village.

---

[41] The recording system was similar to that used at Abu Hureyra. See Moore *et al.* 2000: 96-103.

The archaeological deposits were about one meter deep, as predicted by GPR and anticipated from Korošec' excavations. The top 50 cms consisted of plowsoil, representing at least two major episodes of cultivation in the past. Beneath this were relatively intact levels of the Neolithic settlement. These included areas of irregular stones put down to stabilize the clay surfaces, hearths, and traces of burned daub that were the remains of slight structures. Crossing the trench was a straight stone wall of historic age. There were also a few traces of irregular stone walls in the Neolithic levels. In each deposit from the surface down there were large numbers of potsherds and small quantities of other artifacts, including grinding tools, bone borers, flint tools and waste, and a few pieces of obsidian. Among the potsherds were fragments of several "rhytons," footed vessels with semicircular handles typical of the Danilo culture.

One informal burial of a young child was found in these intact Neolithic deposits, a rare find at Danilo (Level 7, object number DA05 A86). A few other human bones were also recovered.

At the bottom of the trench there was one pit dug into the subsoil full of occupation debris and hearths. This pit was 40 cms deep.

In the 2005 season we excavated five trenches, located across the central portion of this very extensive site in zones that the GPR survey had indicated would be rich in subsurface features. The trenches were spaced up to 100 m apart. Each trench had an upper level of soil of varying thickness disturbed through plowing that often had dense concentrations of artifacts. Beneath this were levels of relatively undisturbed occupation with intact features. Other features, usually pits, were dug into the underlying subsoil.

In Trench A we excavated an additional 34.5 m² area beside the 25 m² trench dug in 2004. Several pits had been dug into the subsoil, presumably to extract clay for building. These were filled and covered over with occupation debris. The whole area continued to be occupied intensively, attested by numerous remains of Neolithic features including fragmentary stone walls, hearths, and open spaces with abundant occupation debris (Figure 7).

Figure 7. Danilo, Trench A.
General view of the Neolithic
deposits looking southwest.
Scale 2 m.

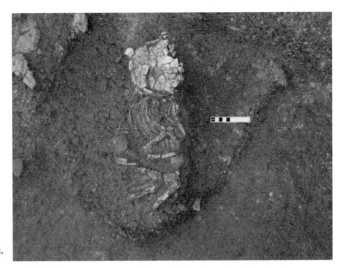

Figure 8. Danilo, Trench A. Burial of a young child (Level 48, object number DA05 A895) beside a hearth, upper left, looking northwest. Scale 10 cm.

In these levels we found a second child burial next to a hearth (Figure 8). Nearer the surface our excavation revealed a further section of the stone wall of historic age that bisected the trench.

Trench B was located at the lower end of Field 1. This 25 m² trench revealed a different sequence of activities. A natural gully in the subsoil had been substantially enlarged by the Neolithic inhabitants to adjust surface drainage (Figure 9). Later, it was partly filled with occupation debris. Then the gully and surrounding area were covered with natural silt that built up as drainage was impeded. Finally, the whole area was covered with a pebble pavement that was laid down to stabilize this sticky, wet surface. This pavement was repaired several times. It seems to have served as an occupation surface as it had several postholes in it and was covered with artifacts, animal bones, and hearths.

Trench C was sited in Field 2, a higher terrace to the northeast of Field 1. This 27.5 m² trench was adjacent to an extensive area excavated by Korešec. As he had found, the initial occupation here consisted of a series of pits and

Figure 9. Danilo, Trench B. The gully. Scale 1 m.

Figure 10. Danilo, Trench C. Pits and postholes dug into the clay subsoil. Scale 1 m.

gullies cut into the subsoil (Figure 10). A few had associated postholes. These features were gradually filled with occupation debris. In a later phase of occupation several stone walls were constructed. At least two of them belonged to a house but the others were probably courtyard or field boundaries.

Danilo is today bisected by a road that was formerly thought to delimit the northwest, or upvalley, side of the site. In the spring of 2004 a contractor had excavated a posthole about 50 m beyond the road to the northwest that had revealed dense Neolithic occupation in the area, so it was clear that the site extended much farther in that direction. Trench D was located in Field 3 just across the road from the rest of the site to explore this sector. An area previously surveyed by GPR in Field 3 had been shown to have subsurface anomalies; this plot was not available for excavation, however. Instead, Trench D was excavated adjacent to the surveyed area and 10 m northeast of the Bitinj well. This 25 m² trench was less productive than the others, despite being surrounded by zones of Neolithic activity. A pond had formed here on the gravel subsoil. In time this was filled with clay. The area had then been occupied by the Neolithic inhabitants who had left hearths and also had paved part of the area to stabilize the surface.

The fifth trench excavated at Danilo, Trench E, was located in a field beside the road on its southeast side, a sector not explored with GPR. Menđušić had excavated a small trench there in 1992 in which he had found traces of a house. We decided to excavate anew in this field to try to expand on the information he had recovered. Furthermore, this field and Field 1 were on opposite sides of a large trench excavated by Korošec, so it was expected that excavations there would illuminate his results. This 32 m² trench was shallower than the others, as the subsoil lay only 0.3 m below the present-day ground surface. Unusually, however, there was less disturbance of the topsoil, probably because of erosion of the ground surface.

Figure 11. Danilo, Trench E. The outline of a rectangular, single-roomed house. Scale 1 m.

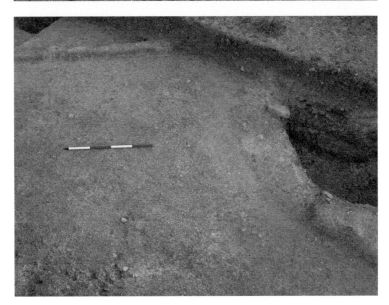

Figure 12. Danilo, Trench E. Stake impressions in the subsoil. Scale 1 m.

The earliest occupation was represented by two large, deep pits. These had a complex history. In their final phase of use their rims were delineated with clay walls, and they seem to have served as a pit dwelling. Contemporary with this late phase of occupation, a rectangular house was built beside the pit dwelling (Figure 11). Although the walls survived only a few centimeters high, it was possible to determine how the structure had been built. First, two parallel lines of stakes were set in place 0.2 m apart along the lines of the walls. The tips of these stakes had been shaped, leaving characteristic impressions in the subsoil (Figure 12). Then brush was forced between the lines of stakes to make a wall. Presumably this structure was held together with withies. Next clay was applied to the surfaces of the wall, and possibly added as a binder within the wall itself. The lines of stake impressions could clearly be seen in the surface of the subsoil, as could the slumped clay of the walls. This is the first such complete Neolithic house excavated in Dalmatia.

The largest single category of artifacts we recovered at Danilo was the potsherds, present in great quantities but much fragmented. All the other artifacts, including bone tools, chipped stone and obsidian, grinding tools and other stone implements, were quite few in number considering the size of the excavated area.

We complemented these excavations with extensive field walking of the site to determine not only its extent but also the intensity of occupation, to the degree that this could be determined by surface finds. While occupation appears to have been continuous across the very considerable area of the site, the density of artifacts and other finds varied from one part to another. This suggests that some areas may have been more heavily used than others.

Danilo Bitinj was much larger than we had anticipated at the start of our research. It is possible, however, that not all the site had been inhabited at the same time, as Korošec himself had suggested.[42] Nearly all the artifacts we recovered from the site were characteristic of the Danilo or Middle Neolithic phase in the Dalmatian cultural sequence. In addition, there was also a little later material present, some of it Roman, not unusual in this locality.[43] A further preliminary observation may be offered: that the structures revealed in each of our trenches were much more varied than we had been led to expect from the data presented in Korošec' reports.

Pokrovik 2004-2006

The site of Pokrovnik lies at the foot of the northwestern end of a limestone ridge, the Mideno brdo, on the southern edge of the modern village. It is situated below the Gradina hill, a prominent landmark, on a shelf that slopes gently away to the northwest. On top of the hill is a church, Sveti Mihovil, and a prehistoric hill-fort or *gradina*. A Hvar culture vessel had been found in a pit just below the top of the hill that is now in the City Museum of Drniš,[44] and we found deposits of occupation material containing Danilo potsherds on the same slopes (Figure 15). This suggests that people began to use the hilltop during the Neolithic. The settlement at Pokrovnik was located to take advantage of the copious Pećina spring that lies at the foot of the hill in a grove of hackberry trees (Figure 4). This is the only perennial spring in the district. In wet weather the spring overflows and a modest stream flows past the northern and western end of the site out to the valley beyond. The gorge of the Čikola River is only 4 km to the north (Figure 13) while the Adriatic, visible from the heights above the site, is 18 km away.

As at Danilo, the soil on the site was grey in color and there was a scatter of daub and occasional artifacts across the surface. Thus, it was relatively easy to delimit the extent of prehistoric occupation. From this, we estimated that the core of the site covered about

---

[42] Korošec 1958-1959: 148.
[43] The artifacts, animal bones and shells from Danilo Bitinj have been deposited in the City Museum of Šibenik.
[44] Menđušić 1998: 54.

Figure 13. View of the site of Pokrovnik from the Gradina hill looking northwest. The Čikola Gorge is visible in the middle distance.

3 ha, so it had been an unusually substantial village. We need to keep in mind, however, the ample evidence of surface erosion at Pokrovnik. Furthermore, it appeared that the site extended considerably farther to the east under cultivated fields that had covered the archaeological deposits with up to two meters of topsoil. Finds of Neolithic artifacts in this area confirm this probability. It is likely, therefore, that the prehistoric settlement had once been more extensive than it appears today, that is at least 4 ha in extent.

The excavation

The main aim of our research at Pokrovnik in 2006 was to excavate a series of trenches to the subsoil in order to gain more information on the sequence of occupation there. Once again, recovery of substantial samples of plant remains and animal bones to reconstruct the economy was a fundamental objective. A further aim was to explore the setting of the site and its ecology. It is becoming clear that gaining a broader understanding of the adjustments that Neolithic communities made to what was almost certainly a dynamic and changing landscape will be crucial to our project's outcome.

One strip field, 150 m long and 10 m wide, was available for excavation. It lay between the fields in which Brusić had located his trenches, and transected the site from the bottom of the escarpment to the western edge of the inhabited area (Figure 14). We had

Figure 14. Location of the four trenches we excavated in a single field that transected the site.

already surveyed the field with GPR in 2004, so had a good idea of what to expect. The GPR investigations had indicated that there were numerous anomalies down the entire length of the field, suggesting that occupation here had been intense. Erosion had removed an unknown, but presumably substantial, amount of sediment from the surface, exposing the Neolithic levels. Accordingly, the weathered topsoil horizon was relatively shallow. Beneath that, the Neolithic deposits were largely intact and relatively undisturbed.

We excavated four trenches in a line down the field, labeled D, A, C and B respectively (Figure 15). Trenches D and A yielded essentially similar sequences, with up to 1 m of Impressed Ware deposits above the subsoil, overlain by 1 m of Danilo levels. We found the same sequence in Trench C though the deposits here were much thinner. Trench B proved to be beyond the regular area of habitation and so yielded very little material.[45]

Trench D, located towards the top, or southeast end, of the field, was 25 m² in area. The earliest Impressed Ware levels consisted of patches of stones that consolidated the natural surface, itself composed of red clay that had probably washed in during the later Pleistocene. A considerable amount of occupation debris, including artifacts and animal bones, was associated with these levels. Then a massive wall was built from north to south, that is at right angles to the original slope of the site (Figure 16). Similar walls were found

---

[45] A report of excavations carried by another team at Pokrovnik following our campaign (Marijanović 2017) was published too recently to be discussed here.

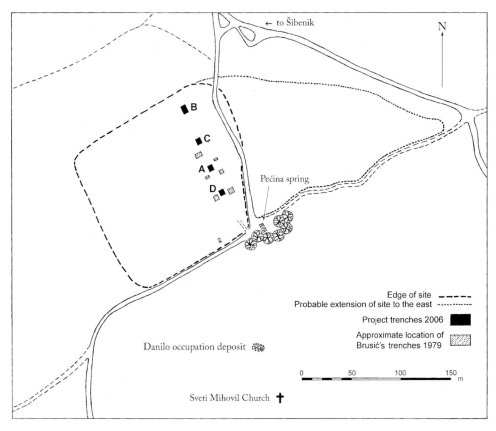

Figure 15. Plan of the site of Pokrovnik showing the locations of the trenches we excavated and also those excavated by Brusić in 1979.

Figure 16. Pokrovnik, Trench D. View of a massive wall in the Impressed Ware levels from the north. Scale 1m.

Figure 17. Pokrovnik, Trench A. View of a massive wall in the Impressed Ware levels and a pit dug from the overlying Danilo phase, looking north. Scales 1m.

in trenches A and C; they appear to be terrace walls across the settlement. Further substantial deposits of occupation debris and large hearths covered the wall. At this point in the sequence there was a gradual transition to the Danilo phase, marked by an increasing mixture of Impressed Ware and Danilo style potsherds.[46] Next, a level of yellow clay covered much of the trench, a feature that also occurred in A. Thereafter, the upper levels, also composed of dense occupation debris, contained largely Danilo material.

Trench A, 30 m² in area, was downhill from D. Here, too, the earliest Impressed Ware habitation consisted of dense layers of occupation debris and hearths on the red clay subsoil. A pit had been cut into the subsoil, possibly to extract clay for building purposes. Then the trench was bisected by a massive wall similar to the one in D. These features were clearly among those that had

created the anomalies that we had detected in the GPR survey. Next, a massive pit was dug through these levels into the subsoil; it was filled later with occupation debris that contained Danilo style pottery (Figure 17). Then the inhabitants laid down a level of yellow clay, as in D. The later stages of settlement here were marked by an accumulation of more occupation debris, traces of walls and many daub fragments from collapsed buildings, as well as pebble pavements that consolidated the sticky surface of the site (Figure 18).

Trench C, also 30 m² in area, was farther downhill from D and A. This trench was shallower than D and A, about 1 m in depth overall. It revealed the same sequence of occupation, an Impressed Ware phase followed by Danilo occupation, but in abbreviated form. The natural surface consisted of exposed limestone bedrock and an area of red clay that had formed from natural wash in a low-lying hollow. On top of this were a few floors and some occupation debris. The rest of the sequence consisted of a series of walls, most of which trended north-south. Again, the most likely interpretation is that these served as terrace walls, this time, however, at the edge of the settlement. There was considerable evidence of

---

[46] McClure *et al.* 2014.

Figure 18. Pokrovnik, Trench A. Interior of a two-roomed house in the Danilo levels, with an exterior pebble pavement to the left of the house wall, looking north. Scale 2m.

wear, probably from the hooves of animals, on the limestone natural surface and on paving associated with the stone walls. So, animals passed along these tracks often. This was not a habitation area for the inhabitants of the site, however.

Trench B was situated towards the bottom end of the field beyond C. We opened up 40 m² there because the GPR survey had indicated that this area was rich in anomalies. For once, however, we were misled by the GPR results. The anomalies proved to be largely geological in character as here the bedrock rises up in a ridge to near the ground surface. There were slight traces of occupation debris, and a few artifacts were recovered. The lack of evidence for structures and the scarce indications of human activity indicated, however, that this area was beyond the densely inhabited part of the settlement. The area did yield plentiful large stones and it is these that were recorded in the GPR survey.

We recovered an unusually large accumulation of pottery from all phases of occupation. The Impressed Ware levels yielded few other finds. The exception was a largely intact female clay figurine. This piece was remarkably well made, representing a true art object in the quality of its conception and execution (Figure 19). It came from level 22 at the base of Trench D, thus slightly after the founding of the site. This level is securely dated to 7090 ± 25 BP (PSU-5293/UCI-AMS-116205), that is c. 8000 cal BP (6000 cal BC[47]). Otherwise, there were a few chipped stone and other stone tools. In contrast, the Danilo

Figure 19. Pokrovnik, Trench D. A seated baked clay female figurine from the Impressed Ware levels. (Level 22, object number PK06 D380; Scale 5 cm.)

---

[47] McClure et al. 2014: Table 1, Figure 4.

levels had some more chipped stone, plenty of bone tools, and some other stone tools. In addition, in the Danilo levels we found a little obsidian and marine shell.[48] Thus, the evidence for maritime contact was largely confined to the upper levels. This is a counterintuitive observation given that it has long been thought that it was during the Impressed Ware phase that the inhabitants of this region and much of the rest of the Mediterranean coast were in contact by sea.

Preservation of bone was particularly good, and a large sample of identifiable pieces was recovered. The flotation process proceeded smoothly, using two machines. As a result, large samples of soil from every level that contained charred plant remains were processed. The soil, while still essentially clay, was easier to wash and the number of charred seeds recovered was higher than at Danilo. Thus, we were able to compile a more substantial assemblage of bone and plant material for analysis.

Our trenches gave us a clear view of a cross-section of the settlement towards its center. The site is this area consisted of houses and open areas that were used intensively for human habitation and the activities associated with it. We found traces of houses in the form of clay walls and associated lines of stones, as well as clay floors. The abundant fragments of clay daub provided further evidence of once-existing structures. The terrace walls of the Impressed Ware village would have been a conspicuous feature. All of this amplifies similar evidence recovered by Brusić in the areas he excavated. Our data from the structures and the pottery suggest, however, that the transition from one cultural episode to the next was anything but abrupt. Instead, it seems to have taken a considerable period of time during which up to 0.5 m of occupation deposit accumulated.

Seth Button, then a graduate student from the University of Michigan, carried out a site survey of the vicinity during the 2006 season. He found traces of Neolithic material scattered quite widely, but no occurrence of artifacts of more recent date. This is surprising, given the presence of the *gradina* (hill-fort) and a few other later prehistoric sites in the vicinity. Surface erosion during the Holocene is likely to have been a factor here.

Button also conducted a site catchment analysis[49] with our geological team. This extended in a two-kilometer radius out from the site. Pokrovnik was a long-lived agricultural village, ranged along the side of a dry valley at the foot of a line of hills. There is ready access on foot to the ridge to the east. Thus, almost half the catchment of the site consists of rough limestone hill country, covered today by scrub vegetation with only a few scattered cultivated plots. The local farmers regard it as poor land for grazing. On the west the site opens onto gentle sloping terrain now divided into large fields but with thin soil cover for the most part. This would not appear immediately to be an optimal location for the large farming village that we know flourished through two major phases of the Neolithic, a paradox that calls for further investigation.

---

[48] The artifacts, animal bones and shells from Pokrovnik have been deposited in the City Museum of Drniš.
[49] Higgs and Vita-Finzi 1972: 27.

The location of Pokrovnik contrasts markedly with Danilo, an even more extensive site located in the center of a fertile valley surrounded by arable land. We need to ask, therefore why these sites were established in such different locations, and what impact this might have had on their economies as well as other aspects of life. One factor does seem to have been of prime importance, the availability of water. The Danilo Valley has a high water table and streams form on the surface in the winter. Pokrovnik, on the other hand, lies in an area with only one source of water in the present day, the well at the top of the site. If this was the main, or even only, source of water in the past, it would have been a major element of attraction in an otherwise dry landscape.

The site of Pokrovnik has archaeological deposits up to two meters deep, and these are very little disturbed. This is in contrast with the otherwise apparently heavily eroded surroundings of the site. Smith suggests that it may actually lie in a large sinkhole, a hypothesis supported by the evidence from Trench B, and that this would account for the depth of the deposits. Preservation on the site itself is much better than at Danilo and the soil seems to have been less destructive of organic material. The sequence of occupation recovered in our trenches matched that of Brusić's excavations, a solid deposit of Impressed Ware with Danilo occupation on top, and traces of Hvar, or Late Neolithic, material near the surface. Surprisingly, given the presence of the well, we found no later material in our trenches or on the surface in the surrounding countryside, in contrast with Danilo.

Chronology of Pokrovnik and Danilo

Our objective has been to establish a comprehensive chronology for both sites based exclusively on AMS dates. Given the paucity of radiocarbon dates from elsewhere in the region, this represents an important step in developing a firm chronology for the arrival and subsequent development of farming societies in the Adriatic Basin through the Neolithic. To this end, we have obtained dates from nearly all the trenches excavated at each site. In several instances these include sequences of dates covering the entire occupation. To date there are 12 dates from Pokrovnik and 14 from Danilo. From these data we have determined the duration of occupation at each site and have formed a preliminary judgment on how these villages developed through time. The dates are listed in Table 1.[50]

Pokrovnik was founded *c.* 8000 cal BP (*c.* 6000 cal BC) based on three dates from levels 23, 22, and 21 in Trench D (PSU-5556/UCIAMS-119837: 6975 ± 30 BP, PSU-5293/UCIAMS-116205: 7090 ± 25 BP, OxA-17194: 6999 ± 37 BP). This is a minimum estimate, given that occupation will have begun a little before the age of the samples selected for dating. The most recent dates from the site are from Trench C level 7 (OxA-17124: 6197 ± 39 BP) and Trench D level 3 (OxA-17223: 6170 ± 35 BP), that is around 7100 cal BP, 5100 cal BC. The surface of the site had been eroded and Hvar pottery was recovered from the excavations so the site was inhabited for at least a century or two later than these dates. We estimate that occupation continued there until after *c.* 7000 cal BP (*c.* 5000 cal BC). Thus, the village was inhabited for the entire seventh millennium BP (fifth millennium cal BC) and beyond. A Bayesian analysis of the dates from Trench D confirms this chronology.[51] Given the spread of dates from Trenches A, C and D it appears that occupation was continuous in the central part of the site that we excavated.

The duration of occupation at Danilo, at least in the areas of the site that we excavated, was much shorter. The earliest date is OxA- 14449: 6284 ± 40 BP from Trench A level 17 and the latest OxA-15680: 5987 ± 35 BP from Trench B level 21. Thus, the chronological range is from c. 7220 to 6830 cal BP (c. 5300 to 4900 cal BC). These dates provide a minimum duration of occupation of about 400 calendar years. Again, as the surface of the site had been heavily eroded, occupation there would have continued for longer. The dates have been obtained

---

[50] Calibrated with OxCal v4.2.3 Bronk Ramsey 2009; r:5 IntCAl13 atmospheric curve, Reimer *et al.* 2013.
[51] McClure *et al.* 2014: Figure 7.

from four of the five trenches we excavated. They indicate that all of the areas tested were inhabited at the same time.[52]

Table 1. AMS radiocarbon dates from Pokrovnik and Danilo.

Site; Sample #	Trench/ Level	Material	Laboratory #	¹⁴C BP	2σ cal B.C.E.
Pokrovnik	A/8	*Triticum monococcum* (einkorn) charred grain	OxA-17195	6626 ± 39	5625-5490
Pokrovnik	A/33	*Triticum dicoccum* (emmer) charred grain	OxA-17328	6810 ± 40	5755-5630
Pokrovnik	C/7	*Triticum dicoccum* (emmer) charred grain	OxA-17124	6197 ± 39	5295-5240 (7.9%) 5235-5040 (87.5%)
Pokrovnik	C/23	*Triticum dicoccum* (emmer) charred grain	OxA-17125	6568 ± 36	5615-5585 (9.1%) 5570-5475 (86.3%)
Pokrovnik	D/3	*Triticum dicoccum* (emmer) charred grain	OxA-17223	6170 ± 35	5220-5015
Pokrovnik PK-44	D/9	*Ovis aries* (sheep) >30kDa gelatin	PSU-4960/ UCIAMS-106477	6280 ± 20	5310-5215
Pokrovnik PK-39	D/10	*Bos taurus* (cow) >30kDa gelatin	PSU-5294/ UCIAMS-116206	6190 ± 25	5220-5055
Pokrovnik	D/11	*Triticum dicoccum* (emmer) charred grain	OxA-17193	6625 ± 36	5625-5490
Pokrovnik PK-45	D/11	*Ovis aries* (sheep) >30kDa gelatin	PSU-4961/ UCIAMS-106478	6840 ± 25	5765-5660
Pokrovnik	D/21	*Triticum monococcum* (einkorn) charred grain	OxA-17194	6999 ± 37	5985-5785
Pokrovnik PK-7	D/22	*Bos taurus* (cow) >30kDa gelatin	PSU-5293/ UCIAMS-116205	7090 ± 25	6025-5965 (56.3%) 5960-5905 (39.1%)
Pokrovnik PK-15	D/23	*Ovis aries* (sheep)	PSU-5556/ UCIAMS-119837	6975 ± 30	5980-5945 (8.3%) 5920-5760 (87.1%)
Danilo Bitinj	A/14	*Triticum monococcum* (einkorn) charred grain	OxA-17196	6212 ± 35	5300-5190 (34.4%) 5185-5055 (61%)
Danilo Bitinj	A/17	*Ovis musimon* (sheep) right calcaneum	OxA-14449	6284 ± 40	5365-5205 (94.2%) 5160-5150 (0.3%) 5145-5135 (0.3%) 5095-5080 (0.7%)
Danilo Bitinj	A/31	*Triticum dicoccum* (emmer) charred grain	OxA-15764	6226 ± 37	5305-5195 (50%) 5180-5060 (45.4%)

---

[52] For a more extended discussion of these dates and their regional implications, see McClure *et al.* 2014.

Site; Sample #	Trench/ Level	Material	Laboratory #	¹⁴C BP	2σ cal B.C.E.
Danilo Bitinj	A/36	*Triticum monococcum* (einkorn) charred grain	OxA-17197	6121 ± 37	5210-4955
Danilo Bitinj DA-6	A/42	*Ovis aries* (sheep) >30kDa gelatin	PSU-5290/ UCIAMS-116202	6155 ± 25	5215-5025
Danilo- Bitinj	A/46	*Triticum dicoccum* (emmer) charred grain	OxA-15681	6180 ± 34	5225-5020
Danilo Bitinj	B/6	*Rosa* sp. (wild rose) charred seed	OxA-17329	6204 ± 38	5295-5050
Danilo Bitinj	B/21	*Triticum monococcum* (einkorn) charred grain	OxA-15680	5987 ± 35	4985-4785
Danilo Bitinj	B/24	*Rosa* sp. (wild rose) charred seed	OxA-17198	6093 ± 36	5210-5145 (10.2%) 5140-5095 (2.7%) 5085-4905 (82%) 4865-4855 (0.5%)
Danilo Bitinj	B/24	*Rosa* sp. (wild rose) charred seed	OxA-17199	6103 ± 37	5210-5090 (21.9%) 5085-4935 (73.5%)
Danilo Bitinj	C/7	*Rosa* sp. (wild rose) charred seed	OxA-17200	6161 ± 36	5215-5005
Danilo Bitinj	C/15	Rosa sp. (wild rose) charred seed	OxA-17224	6083 ± 35	5210-5165 (5.6%) 5080-4895 (88.1%) 4870-4850 (1.8%)
Danilo Bitinj	E/5	*Triticum monococcum* (einkorn) charred grain	OxA-17126	6237 ± 37	5310-5200 (63.2%) 5180-5065 (32.2%)
Danilo Bitinj	E/14	*Triticum monococcum* (einkorn) charred grain	OxA-15765	6245 ± 39	5315-5200 (70.1%) 5175-5070 (25.3%)

Pottery from Pokrovnik and Danilo

Excavations at Danilo Bitinj and Pokrovnik revealed that these sites provide excellent case studies of the development of pottery in the Eastern Adriatic during the Early and Middle Neolithic. The Early Neolithic in this eastern Adriatic region (as well as in a large part of the central and western Mediterranean coasts) is characterized by *Impresso* ware, considered characteristic of the *Impresso* or Impressed Ware culture. Basic forms of both coarse and fine ware are deep, ovoid, spherical and hemispherical vessels (pots, bowls and, more rarely, cups; Figure 20) that are often quite large.[53] Surface colors vary from pale brown to dark brown and dark grey. Vessels are usually closed forms with inverted rims and simple rounded lips (Figure 20: 1, 3, 5). Slightly everted rims, which give the vessels' profiles an S-form, are more rare (Figure 20: 2, 4). A large number of fragments are decorated with impressed patterns created with the edges or points of different objects. Impressed motifs often cover the outer surface entirely, either in irregular patterns or grouped in horizontally or vertically oriented rows or zigzags. Most commonly vessels are ornamented by one motif/technique only. On some more finely made vessels, the decoration is applied by a comb and/or roulette (Figure 20: 3). In later phases of the *Impresso* ware, a *tremolo* technique is also used on some finely made vessels (Figure 20: 4).

Danilo wares, characteristic of the Danilo culture, characterize the Middle Neolithic along a long stretch of the eastern Adriatic coastline and its hinterland. This pottery shows a far larger diversity of vessel shapes and ornamental styles than the more conservative *Impresso* wares.[54] Among its coarse ware, spherical, inverted pots prevail (Figure 21: 1), although large open bowls also occur. Most of the coarse ware lacks decoration. The bearer of the distinguishing Danilo style is fine ware, dark gray or black in color, and with a burnished surface. Most typical are hemispherical, slightly closed bowls, with externally thickened rims (Figure 21: 6, 7). Deep or shallow biconical bowls and plates with more strongly everted rims are also common (Figure 21: 8-10). Somewhat deeper rounded bowls have elongated necks and an S-profile (Figure 21: 4). The main decorative technique is incision, and motifs vary from linear (groups of parallel lines, rows of triangles, net-like motifs; Figure 21: 3,

---

[53] For the typology of *Impresso culture wares in Dalmatia* see Batović 1966: 53-68; Batović 1979: 499-500, 503-509; Brusić 1994-1995: 4-8; Brusić 2008: 37-46; Čečuk and Radić 2005: 71-77; Marijanović 2005: 30-31; Marijanović 2009; Müller 1994.

[54] For the typology of Danilo culture wares see Batović 1979: 540-548; Brusić 2008: 54-56; Korošec 1958-1959: 40-93; Korošec 1964: 33-49; Korošec and Korošec 1974: 16-22.

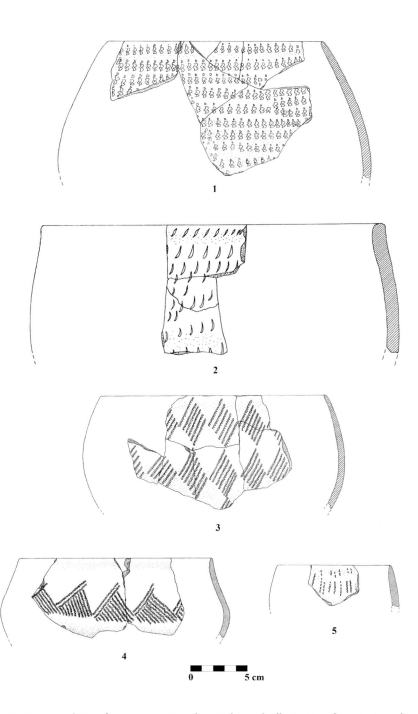

Figure 20. Impressed Ware/Impresso pottery from Pokrovnik, illustrating characteristic shapes and decoration.

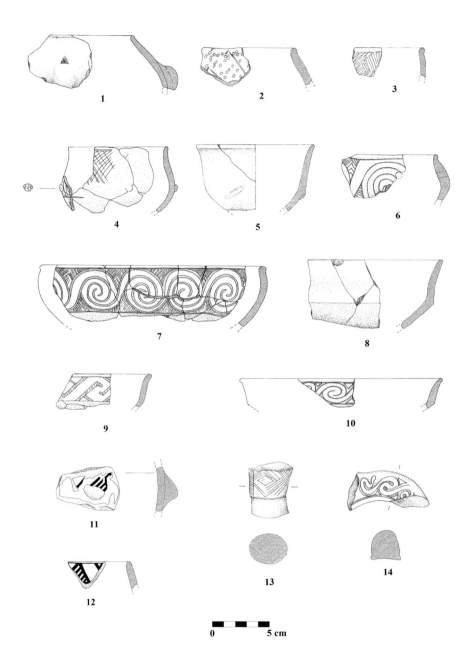

Figure 21. Danilo pottery from Pokrovnik and Danilo, illustrating characteristic shapes and decoration.

4) to curvilinear (in particular spirals). Impression is used more rarely, mainly combined with incisions (Figure 21: 2). Hemispherical and biconical bowls are mostly decorated by a strip of "running" spirals whose incisions are filled with red paste (Figure 21: 6, 7, 10). On some examples the spiral is replaced by an angular-meander variant (Figure 21: 9). Both coarse and fine wares are sometimes decorated with circular or oval relief appliqués, of which schematized zoomorphic examples (e.g., animal's head) are particularly interesting (Figure 21: 4, 5, 11). Some Danilo vessels also have strap or lug handles (Figure 21: 1).

Painted pottery forms a distinctive category of Danilo's fine ware. In the archaeological literature, this kind of pottery is known as *Figulina* ware and is found widely distributed in the Adriatic coastal regions.[55] Analysis of *Figulina* vessels from Pokrovnik and Danilo suggests that, despite the similarities in this pottery among widely-distributed sites, they were made locally.[56] These painted vessels are found in many open and closed shapes (e.g., pots, bowls, cups and plates) and are usually made of fine-grained, purified clay, fired in an oxidized atmosphere resulting in light red, pink and orange hues. The decoration is applied with a brush and the painted pigment is usually dark brown, gray or black. Motifs are most frequently linear (rows of triangles or groups of parallel lines; Figure 21: 11, 12). Finally, other vessels often classified as cult objects are also made of fired clay; the most commonly found are legs and handles of so-called rhytons or *rhyta* (Figure 21: 13, 14).

---

[55] Spataro 2009.
[56] Teoh *et al.* 2014, 357.

Pottery and the Early Farming
in Dalmatia Project

The pottery from Danilo Bitinj and Pokrovnik fits well into the established typologies of *Impresso* and Danilo Neolithic phases. Pottery analysis at Pokrovnik and Danilo Bitinj provides an opportunity to study ceramic use and manufacture at two open-air Neolithic villages throughout a millennium. The pottery from these sites is highly fragmented and numerous: over 1,500 kg of pottery was recovered from the two sites and all of it is currently being studied. The results presented here are based on preliminary analysis of pottery from Trench E at Danilo Bitinj and Trench D (lower levels) at Pokrovnik. These findings are only first glimpses at the diversity of pottery styles and technologies at these two sites. Future analyses of this pottery will concentrate on a more comprehensive study of pottery manufacture, and local developments of pottery technology, typology, style, and function.

Danilo Bitinj, Trench E

All pottery fragments (n=3,374) from 19 levels in Trench E were analyzed, and of these 49 individual vessels were identified using a standard Minimum Number of Individuals (MNI) measure. The number of identified vessels is very conservative, since only fragments with clear typological information or other defining characteristics were separated. In the following, we present data for fragments and vessels.

Decoration

The bulk of fragments were undecorated, with only a small percentage, ranging from 0.1-6.7% decorated (Table 2). Decorated fragments were mostly incised (73%) with a variety of other decorative techniques, such as painting, combing and impression also documented (Table 3). Furthermore, 1.6 - 9.4% of pottery sherds were *Figulina* ware. The number of decorated fragments and *Figulina* ware varied by level, largely mirroring relative numbers of pottery fragments from levels (Table 2).

Table 2. Danilo Trench E pottery fragments.

Level	Total	Undecorated	*Figulina*	Fig %	Decorated	Dec %
1	54	47	7	13	0	0
2	134	124	5	3.7	5	3.7
3	182	176	3	1.6	3	1.6
4	43	43	0	0	0	0
5	26	26	0	0	0	0
6	501	457	33	6.6	11	2.2
7	114	106	2	1.8	6	5.2
8	5	5	0	0	0	0
9	36	33	2	5.6	1	2.8
10	36	36	0	0	0	0
11	793	719	56	7.1	18	2.7
12	136	128	4	2.9	4	2.9
13	298	278	18	6	2	0.7
14	555	498	52	9.4	5	0.1
15	1	1	0	0	0	0
16	30	27	1	3.3	2	6.7
17	42	42	0	0	0	0
18	0	0	0	0	0	0
19	339	307	30	8.8	2	0.6
Total	**3325**	**3053**	**213**	**6.4**	**59**	**1.8**

Table 3. Decorations recorded among fragments at Danilo, Trench E.

Decoration	Number	Percent
1.1 (lugs- small)	3	5
1.2 (lug-pill)	2	4
1.3 (lug-button)	1	2
2.1 (smooth cordon)	1	2
4.3 (punch impression)	1	2
4.6 (indeterminate impression)	1	2
5 (incised)	41	73
7 (combed)	1	2
8 (painted or slipped)	1	2
8.1 (painted)	4	6
Total	**56**	**100**

Typology

Due to the fragmentary nature of the assemblage, relatively little typological information is available. Among the fragments, a few vessel forms were identifiable, and data on lip, rim, handle, and base shape were recorded (Table 4). Ten types of lip shapes were documented on 207 fragments in the assemblage, although simple rounded (type 1), rounded edged (type 3.2), and rounded - externally thickened (type 5.2), were the most prevalent. A total of 206 rims were analyzed, and of these, the majority were undifferentiated (73%), with a considerable number also everted (21%). Only 14 handles, largely strap handles (50%), were recorded. A total of 13 bases were present in the assemblage and were comprised of flat bases (31%) and footed bases (69%). Finally, 18 fragments were identified as deriving from carinated forms, either a bowl or jar.

In contrast, twenty vessels were sufficiently large to classify typologically. A hierarchical classification system was utilized to identify group membership of individual vessels. Vessel class is based on the distinction between open and closed vessels, and subdivisions are defined by the Depth Index (Id, maximum diameter by height). Based on this typological system, two vessels are shallow platters or plates (with a depth index of less than 0.45). Seven vessels are bowls (Id: 0.45 - 0.7) and of these, one is a bowl with simple profile, one with a compound profile, and one with a differentiated rim. Six vessels are larger and deeper (Id>0.7), four of which are ollas. Finally, four 'micro-vessels' were identified with diameters and vessel heights of less than 10 cm. In addition, one little bottle with a differentiated rim was identified.

Table 4. Lips, rims, handles and bases on fragments from Danilo Trench E.

Lips	Number	Percent
1 round	68	33
2 flat	7	3
3.1 angular edge	2	1
3.2 rounded edge	52	25
4.4 rounded – internally thickened	1	0.5
5.2 rounded – externally thickened	72	35
5.3 rounded – externally lengthened	1	0.5
5.4 rounded – internally lengthened	2	1
6.2 rounded – double thickened	1	0.5
6.3 lengthened – double thickened	1	0.5
Rims		
0 undifferentiated	150	73
1 straight/flaring inward	9	4

2 flaring outward	44	21
5 rounded inward	3	2
Handles		
0 indeterminate	1	7
3 lugs	2	14
5 tabs	2	14
5.1 pierced tabs	1	7
11 strap	5	36
11.2 vertical strap	2	14
15 bases	1	7
Bases		
4 flat	4	31
5 footed	9	69

Ceramic technology at Danilo Bitinj, Trench E

The 49 vessels were further analyzed using a 10X hand lens and binocular microscope for traces of the manufacturing sequence and to characterize ceramic fabrics. The pottery at Danilo Bitinj is hand-built and, like most prehistoric pottery, is made by pinching, coiling, slab-building or a combination of these. The fragments in this assemblage were too small to identify primary manufacturing techniques. However, a number of variables are commonly documented to describe the manufacturing process, such as surface treatments and firing atmospheres. Due to the fragmentary nature of the pottery, production marks or cracks due to firing or use were not reliable. Table 5 summarizes a few manufacturing characteristics for vessels found in Trench E. Most of the vessels were fine or medium walled, with only few examples of thick-walled pots. Surfaces were carefully finished: 86% of vessels were well-smoothed or polished/burnished on the exterior and 74% on the interior. Finally, firing varied between oxidizing and reducing atmospheres, with a majority of vessels oxidized.

Ceramic fabrics at Danilo Bitinj are fairly diverse. Inclusions (mostly calcite) were largely medium-grained (67%) and numerous in pastes, with 78% of vessels displaying frequencies of 20% or 30%. Sorting was fair to good - inclusions were uniform in size within the paste, with few or no larger inclusions. This suggests that potters prepared clays and inclusions well, perhaps even sifting or screening naturally occurring debris from the clays before creating the fabrics. Despite these similarities, however, paste texture varied from smooth to hackly. Texture is a variable that is dependent on the interplay of clay and inclusions. Given the general uniformity of inclusions, differences in texture are likely due to the properties of the clay, suggesting that perhaps different clays were used. This is a hypothesis that can be tested in the future.

Table 5. Manufacturing and paste characteristics at Danilo, Trench E (n=49; except where noted).

Variable	Type	Number	Percent
Size group	Fine (<6.5mm)	19	39
	Medium (6.5-9mm)	25	51
	Thick (>9mm)	2	4
	n/a	3	6
Kind exterior	Smoothed	7	14
	Well-smoothed	22	45
	Polished/burnished	20	41
Kind interior	n/a	4	8
	Smoothed	9	18
	Well smoothed	19	39
	Polished/burnished	17	35
Firing Atmosphere	Unidentifiable	11	22
	Oxidized	25	51
	Reduced	13	27
Inclusion size (n=33)	Unknown	7	21
	Medium (1/4-1/2mm)	22	67
	Coarse (1/2-1mm)	4	12
Inclusion Frequency (n=32)	Unknown	5	16
	5%	1	3
	10%	1	3
	20%	18	56
	30%	7	22
Sorting (n=32)	Unknown	5	16
	Very Poor	0	0
	Poor	2	6
	Fair	16	50
	Good	9	28
Texture (n=39)	Unknown	9	23
	Smooth	1	3
	Fine	7	18
	Irregular	20	51
	Hackly	2	5

Pokrovnik, Trench D

Only the three deepest levels at Pokrovnik have been studied so far, totaling 2,231 pottery fragments. This assemblage is of particular interest because it is some of the earliest pottery from Dalmatia, and part of the Impressed Ware phenomenon found throughout the Adriatic and western Mediterranean. Although data presented here are preliminary, the diversity of decorative types and sheer quantity of pottery from this stratified site will allow us to to study changes in pottery technology, manufacture, and style through time. Furthermore, detailed study of the contexts of recovery will provide insights into taphonomy and activity areas within this early farming community. Since later levels at Pokrovnik are contemporary with Danilo Bitinj, future analysis will also provide an interesting comparison between the two sites.

Table 6 presents the relative proportions of decorated and undecorated fragments from the three lowest levels at Pokrovnik, and Table 7 specifies decorative techniques identified. Because *Impresso* wares typically have decorations that span much of the surface areas of vessels, decorated fragments are much more common than during the Danilo phase. In contrast, data from Danilo Bitinj, Trench E, show only 8.2% of fragments evidencing decorations (including *Figulina* wares) compared to 50% of the *Impresso* wares at Pokrovnik. Twenty different types of decoration are identified in the three levels, 16 of which are *Impresso* techniques representing 90% of the decorated fragments.

Table 6. Pokrovnik, Trench D pottery fragments.

Level	Total	Undecorated	Decorated	Dec %
21	1135	613	522	46
22	886	424	462	52
23	210	80	130	62
Total	**2231**	**1117**	**1114**	**50**

Table 7. Decorative techniques in Pokrovnik, Trench D, lower levels.

Decoration	Number	Percent
3.1 Cardium impression – edge	253	23
3.3 Cardium impression – stamp and drag	2	0.2
4.1 non-denticulated shell impression	67	6
4.2 linear dentate impression	35	3
4.3 punch impression	55	5
4.4 point and drag impression	1	0.1
4.6 indeterminate impression	82	7
4.8 spatula impression	200	18

4.9 stamped impression	19	2
4.10 continuous impression	9	1
4.11 tooth impression	63	6
4.12 roulette impression	25	2
4.14 triangular tool impression	97	9
4.15 cuneiform impression	5	0.4
4.16 denticulated shell impression (non-Cardium)	21	2
4.17 split impression	69	7
Total Impressions	**1003**	**90**
5 incision	92	8
8 paint or slip	2	0.2
8.1 paint	4	0.4
11.1 figulina	13	1
Total	**1114**	**100**

Evidence from the pottery for dairying at Pokrovnik and Danilo Bitinj

Stable carbon isotope analyses of individual fatty acids in pottery residues from Pokrovnik and Danilo Bitinj revealed the contents of *Impresso* and Danilo period pottery, including the earliest evidence for cheese production in the Mediterranean.[57] Potsherds were selected for analysis from Pokrovnik (n=27) and Danilo Bitinj (n=20). The *Impresso* (n=10), typical Danilo ware (n=20), and *Figulina* (n=9) samples were selected from the unwashed portion of the pottery assemblage from each site. In addition, we analyzed fragments of rhyta (n=4) and sieves (n=4) from previously washed assemblages.

Of the 47 potsherds, 36 (77%) yielded identifiable biomarkers and overall lipid abundances were generally high, likely due to the use of recently excavated and unwashed samples. Ruminant meat and milk fats were identified using general palmitic and stearic fatty acids (16:0 and 18:0, respectively) to distinguish lipids derived from these sources, as well as cheese and fermented dairy products.[58]

Most of the *Impresso* Wares (n=6) contained lipids that indicate ruminant adipose fats, i.e., a 'meat signal'. In addition, two vessels sampled contained signatures that suggest freshwater fish, a very interesting find since the faunal remains from Pokrovnik do not contain any fish bone, nor are there fishing-related artifacts such as fish hooks or line sinkers to indicate fishing as part of a subsistence strategy. Notably, one *Impresso* vessel (#42) had signatures consistent with unfermented dairy fats, i.e., a 'milk signal'. This is consistent with other

---

[57] McClure *et al.* 2018.
[58] Methods are described in detail in McClure *et al.* 2018.

residue studies on early Neolithic pottery in the Balkans and Anatolia.[59] A radiocarbon date from this level at Pokrovnik, Trench D (level 14), dates to 5715-5576 cal BC.[60]

The results of residue analysis of Middle Neolithic wares were more varied and had clear functional distinctions between ceramic types. The majority of the coarser Danilo wares (n=10) had ruminant adipose (meat) and freshwater fish signatures, while two vessels contained milk. These results parallel the *Impresso* ware residues. However, the high-fired *Figulina* wares (n=8) only contained unfermented ruminant dairy fats, i.e. milk, indicating both a functional and a stylistic difference from the typical Danilo wares. This was unexpected given the suite of samples, and provides significant questions for future research. As outlined in an earlier analysis,[61] we found that *Figulina* – although typically regarded as a Middle Neolithic ceramic type – actually first appears at Pokrovnik in the later phases of the *Impresso* occupation, predating the 'typical' Danilo pottery by a few centuries. The samples analyzed as part of this study were all from clearly Middle Neolithic levels at Pokrovnik and Danilo Bitinj, and residue work on the earlier *Figulina* at Pokrovnik is required to see if these are associated with dairying activities at that point as well. Finally, three of the four *rhyta* tested had residues for secondary dairy products, consistent with cheese, while sieve fragments showed clear signs of fermented dairy products consistent with yogurt or cheese production. This is the earliest documented lipid residue evidence for fermented dairy in the Mediterranean region and among the earliest documented anywhere to date.

An increase in the importance of dairying is also visible in animal management strategies of sheep and goats at Pokrovnik. We carried out an oxygen isotope analysis of sheep and goat teeth from *Impresso* and Danilo levels to determine whether animals moved from the coastal plain to the Dinaric Alps over the course of their first year of life. By incrementally sampling the first molar (M1) and comparing the $\delta^{18}O$ isotopes to modern distributions, we identified a shift in management strategies. During the Early Neolithic animals remained on the coastal plain during the course of the year. Although we cannot determine if they moved along the coastal plain, it is clear that they were not brought to higher altitudes during this period. In addition, the oxygen isotopes indicate that the animals were born in the same season of the year, experiencing seasonal fluctuations in $\delta^{18}O$ isotope levels at the same time of tooth growth. In contrast, several Danilo period samples show fluctuations in isotope levels that are consistent with seasonal transhumance between the coastal plain and the highlands. This indicates that farmers at Pokrovnik managed at least a few animals in this way. Furthermore, the Middle Neolithic animals sampled did not experience seasonal fluctuations in $\delta^{18}O$ at the same time of growth of the tooth, clearly indicating differences in birthing season among the animals tested. The emergence of transhumance as a management strategy and multiple birthing seasons of sheep and goats at Pokrovnik point to a shift in animal management strategies and an additional independent line of evidence for increased investment in dairying during the Middle Neolithic.

---

[59] Evershed *et al.* 2008; Spiteri *et al.* 2016
[60] McClure *et al.* 2018.
[61] McClure *et al.* 2014

Genetic data on Neolithic human remains in Europe demonstrate the prevalence of lactose intolerance among early farming populations.[62] We may ask why then were Neolithic farmers at Pokrovnik and Danilo Bitinj milking their livestock. Fermentation of milk into yogurt and cheese decreases lactose content, making it palatable for lactose intolerant individuals. Yogurt and cheese may well have been produced during the Early Neolithic using baskets, wooden bowls, animal hides or stomachs that do not survive in the archaeological record. However, archaeological evidence from the Middle Neolithic clearly points to increased dairying practices with shifts in ceramic typologies, use, and animal management strategies as outlined above, along with evidence of cheese production in functionally specific pottery vessels. An alternative explanation for milk consumption during the Early Neolithic may focus on life history questions. Since young children are able to digest the sugars in raw milk until after weaning, Early Neolithic dairying may well have been geared towards them. Milk is a relatively pathogen-free and nutrient rich food source, and children with access to milk likely enhanced their chances of survival into adulthood. If this was the case, decreased childhood mortality and earlier weaning leading to decreased birth spacing may help explain the increase in human populations seen during the Neolithic, known as the Neolithic Demographic Transition.[63] The evidence for fermented dairy products by 5200 cal BC indicates that at that time a larger proportion of the population was able to consume dairy products and benefit from their significant nutritional advantages.

Conclusions

The pottery assemblages from Danilo Bitinj and Pokrovnik are vast and hold great potential for characterizing and understanding the lifeways of early farmers on the Dalmatian coast. Although our study of ceramics from these two sites has only just begun, preliminary data suggest that changes in pottery from the Early to Middle Neolithic are significant in typology, technology, style, and function. Future analysis will focus on spatial differences in pottery assemblages within and between sites, examine potential changes in use, and further characterize manufacturing techniques during these periods. These data will bring us closer to characterizing the processes of agricultural inception in Dalmatia and subsequent local developments in social organization, food production and consumption, and ritual activity. Finally, pottery analysis will contribute to our understanding of regional interaction, cultural contacts, and the nature of early farming societies on the Dalmatian coast.

---

[62] Burger *et al.* 2007
[63] Bocquet-Appel 2011

The chipped stone, stone tools and other artifacts

Chipped stone

We recovered 563 pieces of chipped stone from Pokrovnik and 1,959 from Danilo. Obsidian represented 3% of the total assemblage from each site (17 pieces from Pokrovnik and 58 from Danilo). The total quantity of chipped stone was modest, a result of the limited supply of raw material in the vicinity of each site. Nodules of flint have been found on the surface of fields in the Danilo Valley and "*kremen*," the Croatian word for flint, does occur among local placenames. But there are no significant sources of flint in the region, the nearest outcrops being two days' walk away.[64] The artifacts we excavated were mostly manufactured from flint pebbles, presumably collected locally. A few were made on longer blades that came from a more distant source. It has been suggested that this locality was across the Adriatic in the Gargano Peninsula.[65] Most of the flint we recovered had been heavily worked and the pieces were small, another indication of the relative scarcity of this raw material. Ninety three percent of the obsidian pieces (16 from Pokrovnik, 54 from Danilo) came from sources on the island of Lipari; intriguingly, five pieces (one from Pokrovnik, four from Danilo) originated in the Carpathian Mountains.[66] The journey by sea from Lipari to the Adriatic coast near Pokrovnik and Danilo would potentially have stretched over 800 km. Even if part of the route was overland, it would still have been necessary to cross the Adriatic to complete the journey. Evidently, those engaged in this traffic were accomplished seafarers. All the obsidian was recovered from Middle Neolithic or Danilo levels at each site, and none from Impressed Ware deposits. This implies that traffic in obsidian, the main indicator of long-distance exchange, began well after the initial Neolithic settlement of the region.

The percentages of retouched tools to manufacturing waste were different at each site, 39% at Pokrovnik and 29% at Danilo. There are, for the moment, no obvious explanations for this. The percentages of retouched tools are unusually high, however, suggesting that some of the tools, at least, were prepared in other parts of the sites or away from them altogether. The differences within each site were striking, with considerable variations in

---

[64] Perhoč 2009: Figure 2.
[65] Forenbaher and Perhoč 2017.
[66] Tykot 2011.

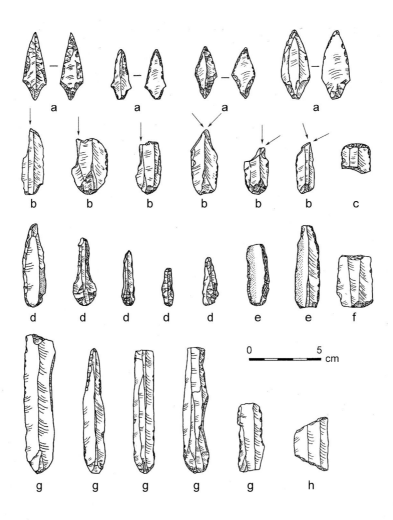

Figure 22. Chipped stone tools from Pokrovnik and Danilo. a, tanged arrowheads; b, burins; c, endscraper; d, borers; e, sickle blades; f, splintered piece; g, blade knives; h, trapezoid.

the quantities of chipped stone recovered from each trench. At Danilo, for example, we recovered 185 pieces from Trench B and 956 from Trench A. This emphasizes that different activities were carried out across the site, and in varying intensities. There seem to have been only modest changes through time, though at Pokrovnik chipped stone was noticeably less abundant in the Impressed Ware levels than in later deposits.

The composition of these assemblages is distinctive (Figure 22). At both sites the most numerous retouched tools were burins, sickle blades, and blade knives. Arrowheads were present in small numbers only. Among the other tools were borers, endscrapers on blades and flake scrapers. There were also a very few microliths, geometric in form, mostly trapezes, and large in size. Nearly all were found in Danilo, or Middle Neolithic, levels but seven were recovered from Impressed Ware levels in Trench D at Pokrovnik. They were unlike microliths found on Mesolithic sites in the region so their presence does not imply continuity in chipped stone technology from the preceding Mesolithic.

The chipped stone waste consisted largely of flakes, in contrast with the tools which were mostly made on blades. There were enough cores, core tablets and crested blades to confirm that the flint tools were manufactured on each site. Many blades had been heat treated to improve their flaking qualities.

In summary, chipped stone tools were made and used only in small quantities at Pokrovnik and Danilo, a direct result of the scarcity of such raw material in the region. The range of tools manufactured was restricted and consisted mostly of tools used for working wood and bone (burins, scrapers), cutting (knives), reaping plants (sickle blades), and probably working leather (scrapers). This is consistent with the evidence we recovered indicating that both villages were inhabited by full-time farmers.

Stone tools

We found stone tools at both sites, though not in large quantities: 116 at Pokrovnik and 119 at Danilo. Nearly all were made on limestone, the ubiquitous bedrock of the region. At Pokrovnik, most of these tools came from the upper, Danilo, levels and there were very few from the lower, Impressed Ware, deposits. As with the flints, there were considerable differences in the numbers of tools recovered from individual trenches. At Danilo, for example, there were only eight such tools in Trench C but 47 in Trench B.

The most numerous tools were grinding dishes, querns, rubbing stones, and mortars (Figure 23). We presume that these were used mainly in food preparation. Considering the intensity with which agriculture was practised, the number of such tools is low. This suggests that much of the food was processed using wooden implements, as was the case in traditional farming in Croatia until recently.

Among the other stone tools were small adzes and axes. Most were made of limestone but a few were of greenstone, probably obtained from Bosnia. These tools were likely used in carpentry. Then there were small numbers of weights, loom weights, balls, hammerstones, spindle whorls, pendants, and beads.

One other category of stone tool was distinctive, the polishers. Most of these were made on carefully-selected water-worn pebbles, probably from the Čikola River and the seashore. At Pokrovnik only, some of the polishers were fashioned from calcite crystals. All these tools had a highly polished rubbing surface, marked with very fine striations. Such tools could have been used to smooth the surfaces of pottery, bone, wood, and leather.

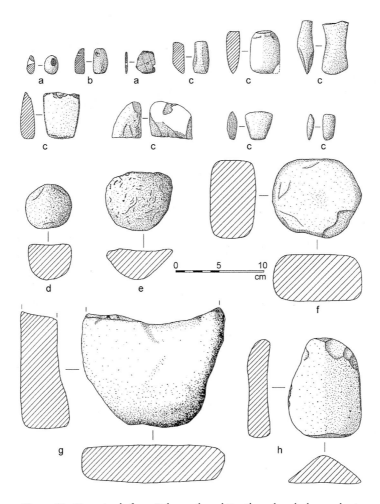

Figure 23. Stone tools from Pokrovnik and Danilo. a, beads; b, pendant; c, adzes; d, stone weight; e, flint chopper; f, rubbing stone; g, quern fragment; h, rubbing stone/chopper.

Bone tools

The bone tools have not yet been examined in detail. We found many more of them at Pokrovnik than at Danilo, a result of the better preservation of such delicate artifacts in the soils at the former site. There were a minimum of 74 bone tools from Pokrovnik and 36 from Danilo. These numbers may increase as the analysis proceeds.

The most common tools at both sites were simple bone points. The rest consisted of awls, spatulae, needles, beads, and a variety of other tools represented by single examples. Most were made on caprine bones. There were also a few antler fragments which were either raw material or in the process of being made into artifacts.

The plant remains from Danilo Bitinj and Pokrovnik

Earlier archaeobotanical studies at the two sites

During the earlier excavations at Danilo in 1953 and 1955 fragments of daub with impressions of cereal grains and chaff were recovered.[67] From latex casts of the impressions Hopf identified four spikelet fragments (i.e. spikelet forks and glumes), a single broken grain of emmer (*Triticum dicoccum*) and three spikelet fragments of einkorn (*Triticum monococcum*). She also tentatively identified one spikelet fragment as naked barley (*Hordeum vulgare* var. *nudum*). The results of these early findings were merely descriptive and no quantitative analysis was possible from so few remains.

At Pokrovnik one small sample (weighing 327 g) excavated by Brusić from the middle Neolithic destruction layer C in trench VI (possibly from a fireplace, although the contextual association was unclear) was dry and wet sieved to maximize recovery of charred plant materials, and 1,698 cereal grains or grain fragments and chaff items were identified.[68] Table 8 lists the species that were recorded in the sample.

The potential for recovery of a more diverse range of taxa was obviously restricted because of the specific nature of the provenance and the size of the samples at both sites. The reported presence during the Middle Neolithic of two glume wheats (and possibly naked

Table 8. The plant species with numbers of specimens recorded by Brusić in his excavations at Pokrovnik.

Species	Grains and Fragments	Chaff (Glume Bases)
Triticum dicoccum	660	68
Triticum monococcum	52	1
Triticum monococcum/dicoccum	908	9

---

[67] Hopf 1964.
[68] Karg and Müller 1990.

barley) was nevertheless important given that archaeobotanical remains had previously not been recorded from any sites of this period in Dalmatia.[69]

Current archaeobotanical studies

The main aims of this study were to determine the range of domestic crops and wild plant resources utilized at the two sites and to assess the extent to which they contributed to overall subsistence economies. The intention also was to compare the development of crop-based agriculture, both at the local and regional scales.

For the recent excavations at Danilo and Pokrovnik sampling strategies were designed to facilitate maximum retrieval of environmental materials, for example charred macro-remains, micro-fauna, and molluscs. Two flotation machines were employed at both sites and this enabled large volumes of excavated deposits to be processed during the 2004-2006 seasons (Table 9). A minimum sample size of 100 l per context/level was set but no maximum limit was defined and much larger volumes were taken in certain areas of the sites (for example as large as 1,290 l: Danilo 2004, Trench A, level 14).

Table 9. Volumes of soil processed by flotation at Pokrovnik and Danilo.

	Volume Floated (l)	Average Sample Size per Level (l)
Pokrovnik: Early Neolithic (n = 26)	3,310	127
Pokrovnik: Middle Neolithic (n = 28)	3,765	135
Danilo: Middle Neolithic (n = 44)	11,120	253

(n = number of samples)

The samples

The quality of preservation and extent of fragmentation of the charred materials varied at both sites from poor (lack of outer cell layers, extreme distortion) to good (cell patterns visible on the testa, minimal deformation), but a majority of the remains was identifiable to the level of genus and species. The numbers of plant items, including whole and fragmentary remains, recovered from each site are given in Table 10. Totals are exclusive of non-seed items, for example parenchymatous tissues, and wood charcoal. Only Trench B at Pokrovnik yielded no identifiable remains other than wood charcoal.

The densities of charred material, measured in terms of numbers of identifiable items per 10 l of sediment floated, were greater at Pokrovnik than at Danilo (overall mean for Pokrovnik was 6.0 items/10 l, n = 54). This trend is reflected in the mean number of taxa (different species and genera) recovered from each site (Table 11), and Danilo had fewer per

---

[69] For a regional review see Borojević et al. 2008: 296-298.

Table 10. Number of identified plant items recovered from Pokrovnik and Danilo.

Site, Period, and Number of Samples	Number of Identified Items	Average Number of Identified Items per 10 l of Sediment
Pokrovnik: Early Neolithic (n = 26)	1,534	4.6
Pokrovnik: Middle Neolithic (n = 28)	2,677	7.1
Danilo: Middle Neolithic (n = 44)	1,892	1.7

Table 11. Average number of identified taxa per phase.

Site, Period, and Number of Samples	Average Number of Identified Taxa per Phase
Pokrovnik: Early Neolithic (n = 26)	7.8
Pokrovnik: Middle Neolithic (n = 28)	6.7
Danilo: Middle Neolithic (n = 44)	4.6

unit volume than for each phase at Pokrovnik – that is, the assemblages were less diverse at Danilo.

There were also variations in density and diversity between the different trenches within each site, and these can be explained in terms of specific activities involving the use of plant resources.[70]

Representation of crops and wild plants

Table 12 lists taxa present in the samples at Danilo and the two phases at Pokrovnik. Most noticeable is the dominance of economic taxa at the two sites: domestic cereals, pulses and oil plants. Wild fruits were recovered from Middle Neolithic levels at both sites and from Early Neolithic levels at Pokrovnik. This demonstrates that plant foods represented a significant component of the subsistence regimes and, more importantly, that crop-based agriculture was established by the Early Neolithic. Wild and/or weed taxa were also identified in samples from both sites.

---

[70] Reed 2006.

Table 12. Taxa identified in samples from Pokrovnik and Danilo.

	Pokrovnik/Impressed	Pokrovnik/Danilo	Danilo
CEREALS			
Hordeum vulgare - grains	+	+	+
Triticum dicoccum - grains	+	+	+
Triticum monococcum - grains	+	+	+
Triticum mono/dicoccum - grains	+	+	+
T. monococcum/dicoccum - chaff	+	+	+
Triticum aestivum (compact type) - grains			+
Triticum spp. (indeterminate) - grains	+	+	+
Panicum miliaceum - grains		+	
cf. *Avena* sp. - grains	+	+	+
Cerealia indeterminate	+	+	+
PULSES + OIL PLANTS			
Linum cf. *usitatissimum*	+	+	+
Lathyrus sativus	+	+	+
cf. *Lathyrus/Pisum* spp.	+	+	
Lens sp.	+	+	+
Large legumes indeterminate	+	+	+
FRUITS			
Pistacia sp.			+
Sambucus sp.	+	+	
Cornus mas	+	+	+
cf. *Cornus sanguinea*	+		+
cf. *Amygdalus* sp.		+	
Rosa cf. *canina*	+	+	+
Rubus sp.	+	+	+
cf. *Sorbus aria*		+	
Vitis sp.		+	
WILD SPECIES			
cf. *Brassica/Sinapis* spp.			+
Caryophyllaceae indeterminate			+
Chenopodium sp.			+
Chenopodiaceae indeterminate	+	+	+
Lolium sp.			+

Gramineae indeterminate	+	+	+
Hypericum sp.	+	+	+
Teucrium sp.	+	+	+
Leguminosae - small	+	+	+
Liliaceae indeterminate	+	+	+
Plantago sp.	+		
Polygonum sp.	+	+	+
Potentilla sp.		+	+
cf. *Verbascum* sp.			+
cf. *Hyoscyamus niger*	+	+	
Urtica urens			+
cf. *Viola* sp.	+		

Cereals

Cereals were the dominant crop type at both sites, both in terms of numbers of remains and ubiquity (percentage presence per site or phase; Figure 24). The three founder crop cereals, hulled barley (*Hordeum vulgare*), einkorn (*Triticum monococcum*) and emmer (*Triticum dicoccum*), were the most frequently occurring species. At Pokrovnik, in both Early and Middle Neolithic phases, emmer was predominant (occurring in over 70% of samples) and grains of hulled barley and einkorn were present in approximately half the samples; at Danilo the grains of all three species were identified in more than 20% of the samples. Einkorn grains were found in large quantities in Trench E at Danilo, and were more numerous than those of emmer and barley recovered from all other trenches at the site. Glume wheat chaff, which could not be identified as to either einkorn or emmer, was found in only a minority of samples and in very low numbers, indicating that processing of the cereals was probably carried out at, or nearby, both sites. Other cereals were far less common in the assemblages; for example, free threshing wheat (*Triticum aestivum* compact type) was found in three samples at Danilo; millet (*Panicum miliaceum*) was present at Pokrovnik in four Middle Neolithic levels; and oats (*Avena* sp.) were tentatively identified at both sites, again in small numbers and in a few samples. Free threshing wheat was a secondary domesticate (that is it evolved at some time after the primary domesticates[71]), and it was integrated in the European Neolithic crop package after the initial dispersal of the founder crops. This was the case also for millet,[72] and so finds of the two taxa in Middle Neolithic levels are consistent with their belated arrival in Dalmatia.

---

[71] Zohary and Hopf 2000: 51-58.
[72] Hunt *et al.* 2008.

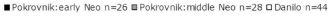

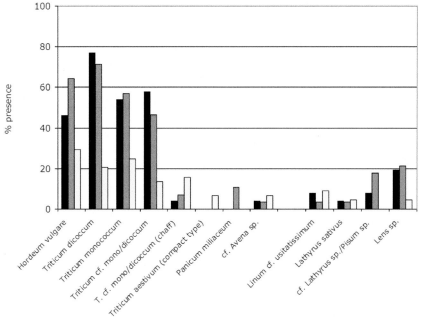

Figure 24. Plant remains from Pokrovnik and Danilo: ubiquity comparisons by phase of cereals, pulses and oil plants.

Pulses and oil plants

Pulses occurred in a few samples at both sites (Figure 24) and the range of taxa represented was limited: only grass pea (*Laythrus sativus*) and lentils (*Lens* sp.) were identified with certainty. Single cotyledons (or fragments of cotyledons) rather than whole pulses were recovered in the assemblages and thus distinction between genera was more problematic; hence the category *Lathyrus/Pisum* sp. (vetchling or vetch/pea) is included in the list of taxa for Early and Middle Neolithic levels at Pokrovnik. Preservation was poor at both sites as indicated by the large quantities of 'indeterminate Leguminosae' fragments (i.e. fragments that were unidentifiable beyond family level) recorded in many samples. Pulses are often under-represented on sites, for example in comparison with cereals. It has previously been assumed this is due largely to the different methods of preparation of the two crop types and the frequency, or otherwise, with which the products or by-products of processing are likely to come into contact with fire in hearths or ovens, thus becoming charred.[73]

Flax seeds (*Linum usitatissimum*) were present at both sites and, as with the pulses, they occurred in only a minority of samples (Figure 24).

---

[73] Dennell 1972: 151; see also Guarino and Sciarrillo 2004.

Grass pea is not included in the list of founder species but was added to the crop repertoire on Neolithic sites in Southeast Europe at an early date.[74] Thus, evidence for its presence in samples from the earliest levels at Pokrovnik is as relevant to consideration of the beginnings of agriculture in Dalmatia as the finds of lentils and flax.

Wild plant foods

The array of fruits and nuts represented at Pokrovnik and Danilo suggests that wild plant resources were also components of the diet during the Early and Middle Neolithic (Figure 25); all would have been growing locally and therefore could have been easily harvested. Wild fruits, which could be eaten raw, dried, cooked or in processed form to remove toxins, were identified in the assemblages from both sites, including elder (*Sambucus* sp.), Cornelian cherry (*Cornus mas*), common dogwood (*Cornus sanguinea*), dog rose/rosehip (*Rosa* cf. *canina*), blackberry/raspberry (*Rubus* sp.) and common whitebeam (cf. *Sorbus aria*). *Rosa* and *Rubus* species are the most commonly occurring taxa at Pokrovnik and at Danilo. Both have numerous seeds (/achenes) per single fruit; rosehips contain more than 100 seeds and blackberries/raspberries have over 50 seeds. The relative abundance of these taxa in the samples is therefore not necessarily a true reflection of their preferential use in comparison with the other fruits, each of which comprises single or very few seeds. Fragments of almond (*Amygdalus* sp.) nutshell and of fruits (/nutlets) of the terebinth/

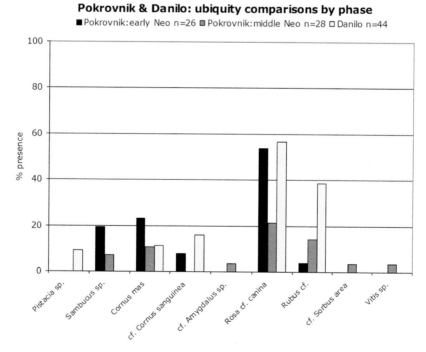

Figure 25. Plant remains from Pokrovnik and Danilo: ubiquity comparisons by phase of fruits.

---

[74] Zohary and Hopf 2000: 120; Colledge and Conolly 2007b.

mastic tree (*Pistacia* cf. *terebinthus/lentiscus/atlantica* spp.) were found in Middle Neolithic levels, the former at Pokrovnik and the latter at Danilo. Wild almonds contain the glycoside amygdalin which is converted into hydrogen cyanide if the fresh seeds (/nuts) are eaten. To render them edible the toxins have to be removed by drying, roasting or leaching.[75] The fruits of *Pistacia* species can be eaten either raw or roasted, and the resins they contain have medicinal properties.[76] One grape pip (*Vitis* sp.), which could not be identified as either wild or cultivated, was found in the Middle Neolithic levels at Pokrovnik. Wild grape pips have previously been recovered from Early, Middle and Late Neolithic sites in Greece,[77] Macedonia,[78] and Italy.[79] Zohary and Hopf note that the wild vines (*Vitis vinifera* subsp. *sylvestris*) are native to southern Europe and their map showing the distribution of the subspecies includes the Dalmatian coast.[80] However, to date there has been no evidence for early finds from the region and so the Pokrovnik grape pip represents important evidence for use of the vine in the Neolithic.

Other wild taxa

Wild or weed taxa were also recovered from the samples at both sites. A majority of these were identified to genus or family level only, thus precluding any definitive ecological interpretations. Several of the taxa represented are likely to have been growing in fields and brought to site with the harvests (for example segetals: *Chenopodium* sp., *Lolium* sp., *Hypericum* sp., *Polygonum* sp.); others possibly inhabited waste ground, perhaps close to the settlements (for example ruderals: *Urtica urens*).

Discussion

Prior to the Early Farming in Dalmatia Project little was known about the nature of crop-based agriculture in the eastern Adriatic. Given its importance as a route via which crops, livestock, techniques and technologies spread into northern Italy and beyond, it is surprising that so few studies have investigated how and when farming was established in the area. Chapman *et al.* have commented that "Dalmatia was a region where the full potential of the archaeological and environmental record had scarcely been realized" due largely to lack of dating evidence and palaeoeconomic data.[81] Prior to the 1990s the absence of environmental evidence, that is the actual remains of domestic plants and animals, on sites in the region was, it seems, due in part to the lack of integrated programs of sampling and flotation; hence pottery was used to demarcate the earliest appearance of the Neolithic and by default it was assumed also that farming was introduced or adopted at the same time.[82] Borojević *et al.* report that before the 1996 excavations at Grapčeva spilja there had been no systematic recovery or investigation of archaeobotanical materials on an eastern

---

[75] Martinoli 2004; Zohary and Hopf 2000: 187.
[76] Jeffrey 1959: 494-5.
[77] Hansen 1991; Housley and Hubbard 2000; Kroll 1979; Renfrew 1989.
[78] Renfrew 1979.
[79] Costantini and Stancanelli 1994; Pals and Voorrips 1979; Rottoli 1999; Rottoli and Pessina 2007.
[80] Zohary and Hopf 2000: 151-159.
[81] Chapman *et al.* 1996: 5-8.
[82] Forenbaher and Miracle 2005.

Adriatic island.[83] Similarly, on the mainland there had been very few sites where the recovery of botanical or faunal remains was an integral part of excavation strategies; for example, the site of Tinj-Podlivade is one of the very few other Neolithic sites in Dalmatia besides Pokrovnik and Danilo with reported archaeobotanical[84] and zooarchaeological data. On the basis of the limited available evidence for the Early and Middle Neolithic it was concluded that that there was a dichotomy between caves and open air settlements in terms of the range of crops and livestock exploited, such that far fewer founder species (i.e. a reduced Neolithic 'package') were identified at the former site type.[85] The present study appears to confirm this, albeit on the basis of limited data from either site type with which to make comparisons, and the suites of crops found at Pokrovnik and Danilo are an indication of the advanced nature of farming from the earliest Neolithic.

The range of domestic species cultivated during the Early Neolithic in Dalmatia shows a marked reduction in diversity in comparison with that recorded for the earliest sites in Greece, where farming first spread to Southeast Europe. In fact, the 'package' of crops present on the Greek sites is similar to that on Pre-Pottery Neolithic sites in Southwest Asia, where the founder species evolved.[86] The Dalmatian evidence reflects the status of the plant economies on Early Neolithic sites to the north and east of the Dinaric Alps, in Bosnia and Herzegovina, Macedonia and Hungary.[87] Bogaard et al. comment that the decrease in diversity indicates a regional trend, "a progressive narrowing of the crop spectrum," from south to north in Southeast Europe.[88] Cultural and/or natural selection pressures may account for this reduced crop package.[89]

---

[83] Borojević et al. 2008: 282.
[84] Huntley 1996: 187-189.
[85] Forenbaher and Miracle 2005: 517; Borojević et al. 2008.
[86] Colledge and Conolly 2007c.
[87] Colledge and Conolly 2007b: 33-34.
[88] Bogaard et al. 2007: 435.
[89] Conolly et al. 2008.

Animal husbandry and environment

Bone preservation and recovery

Animal bone samples can have little meaning unless properly recovered during excavation, and this was given a high priority at Pokrovnik and Danilo. All sediments there were dry sieved through a mesh of 8 mm, excepting only the samples that were selected for water flotation. After that process the washed residues were sorted to recover bone fragments, providing a check against the loss of smaller bones. In practice, the 'dry' sieving retained over 98% of the identifiable mammal and bird bone so that the recovered sample closely reflected what was originally buried.

Most bones were identified in the field, while those of unusual form were later identified with the aid of a reference collection. The bones were measured in a standard manner. In the diagrams below the designations of bone measurements (for example, *Bd*) refer to the standard atlas.[90] The alkaline sediments at both sites ensured good bone preservation, with most of the surface detail retained on each specimen. Each bone was identified to the bone element, side, bone fusion/condition, and species. That part of the bone surviving was recorded by a system of bone 'zones.' Other conditions were also recorded, of burning, gnawing, pathology, and the surface condition of each specimen. This was recorded on a simple five point scale:

1 = bone surface perfect, or nearly so
2 = slight surface erosion
3 = moderate surface erosion; finer detail obliterated
4 = severe erosion; little surface detail remains
5 = amorphous; no surface detail

Table 13 shows that the bone excavated at Danilo was better preserved than that from Pokrovnik. At Danilo, a few percent of the cattle and caprine bones were of condition 1, while none were at Pokrovnik. Nearly 40% of the caprine bones at Pokrovnik fell into condition 3, while at Danilo this was only eight percent of the bones.

---

[90] Driesch 1976.

Table 13. Preservation conditions at the two sites.

Pokrovnik	N	condition 1	condition 2	condition 3	condition 4
pig	11	0	91.0%	9.0%	0
cattle	466	0	91.4%	8.6%	0
caprine	2,470	0	61.5%	38.5%	0

Danilo	N	condition 1	condition 2	condition 3	condition 4
pig	21	0	86.0%	14.0%	0
cattle	275	7.0%	84.5%	8.5%	0
caprine	1,243	2.7%	88.9%	8.1%	0.3%

The faunal remains

Pokrovnik and Danilo have yielded a substantial sample of animal bones and teeth, which together amount to 4,680 identified mammal bones (excluding unidentified fragments), and 976 jaws, jaw fragments and loose teeth. The quality of these samples makes them of particular regional importance because of the scarcity of other, well-recovered collections. In consequence, previous interpretations made about early animal and plant husbandry in Dalmatia are implausible when tested against the Pokrovnik-Danilo sequence.

The relationship between the numbers of excavated animal bones and the animals that they represent can be calculated in several ways. The first of these is by a simple calculation of the proportions of bones from the species as identified: the 'number of identified specimens' (N.isp).

Table 14 shows that caprines, which include both sheep and goat, were by far the most abundant species in all phases, from the earliest Neolithic of the Impressed Ware culture at Pokrovnik through to the upper levels of the Danilo culture at the site of Danilo (Figure 26). However, this is essentially a crude measure of relative abundance, and does not allow for the probability of differential preservation between large and small species, nor for the different numbers of bones in the bodies of different mammalian species. A more accurate

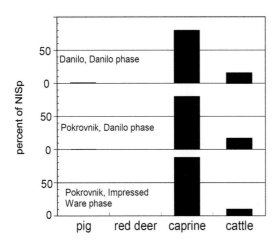

Figure 26. Pokrovnik and Danilo: proportions of main animal species by identified bones.

Table 14. Percentages of species based upon counts of identified bones.

Species	Pokrovnik: Impressed Ware Phase	Pokrovnik: Danilo Phase	Danilo: All Danilo Phase
dog	0.1	0.3	0.7
pig	0.1	0.8	1.2
red deer	0.6	0.5	0.4
caprine (sheep or goat)	88.6	80.5	80.3
cattle	10.6	17.9	17.4
%	100	100	100

Table 15. Proportions of domestic species by mandible count*.

	Pokrovnik		Danilo	
Species	mandibles/teeth	%	mandibles/teeth	%
Pig	1	0.5	3	4.5
Cattle	10	5.3	9	13.4
Caprine	176	94.1	55	82.1
Total	187	100	67	100

(*based upon the number of right or left mandibles for each species, whichever is the greater number)

method lies in calculating proportions based upon the numbers of the better preserved cranial and limb bones from the animals in question. For example, the mandible, distal humerus and distal tibia usually survive well in archaeological animal bone collections, and provide a more secure basis for calculation of relative abundance. This method of calculation is known as the 'minimum number of individuals' (M.ind). At both Danilo and Pokrovnik, the teeth and mandibles show the best survival, and a calculation based on these gives the following numbers and proportions (Table 15):

This calculation gives a rather higher proportion of caprines (Figure 27), due to the lesser survival of the caprine bones when compared with the larger cattle bones. However, by either method the predominance of sheep and goat among the mammal bones is clearly evident. At Pokrovnik, the minimum number of caprines tabulated above is 176, based on the mandibles. There are 2,479 identified caprine bones, giving a ratio of identified mandibles to identified bones of 1:14. At Danilo, the better preservation has allowed more post-cranial bones to survive, with a caprine mandible to bone ratio (to the nearest whole number) of 1:23. The good state of bone preservation at Pokrovnik and Danilo can be compared with that found for caprine bones from sites in Britain and elsewhere, among samples that show the best preservation that Legge has encountered (Table 16).

The surviving part of each identified bone was recorded by a system of zones to enumerate the articular ends (epiphyses) and shafts (diaphyses). The survival of these parts of the individual bones at Pokrovnik is shown in Figure 28. In this diagram, the survival percentage of each bone is plotted by right against left, 100% being the minimum number of individuals indicated by the survival of 176 left mandibles or part-mandibles. Limb bone shaft fragments show a high survival (tibia, radius, humerus) as do early fusing articular ends such as the proximal radius and distal humerus. These bones have high density, while late fusing bones such as the proximal tibia, distal radius, proximal humerus, and distal femur are of low density and show only 4-5% survival. Atypically, the proximal femur shows a high rate of survival. Many proximal femurs survive as unfused articular ends, which is likely to relate to a particular butchery practice. The diagram shows the extent to which mid-shaft sections of limb bones may survive rather better than the articular ends of the same bones.

Table 16. Ratio of identified caprine mandibles to identified limb bones at various sites.

Site	Ratio	Preservation Conditions
Grimes Graves (UK)	1:30	Excellent; protected midden
Runnymede (UK)	1:31	Excellent; protected midden
Down Farm (UK)	1:3	poor; dispersed bones
Pokrovnik	1:14	good; dispersed bones
Danilo	1:23	very good: dispersed bones

(Grimes Graves (UK)[91], Runnymede (UK)[92], Down Farm (UK)[93], Pokrovnik[94], Danilo[95])

---

[91] Legge 1992.
[92] Serjeantson 2006 and pers. comm.
[93] Legge 1991a, 1991b.
[94] This study.
[95] This study.

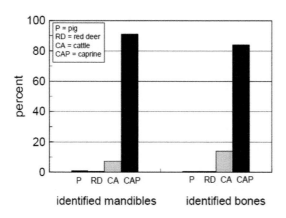

Figure 27. Pokrovnik: proportions of main animal species from all identified bones and jaws.

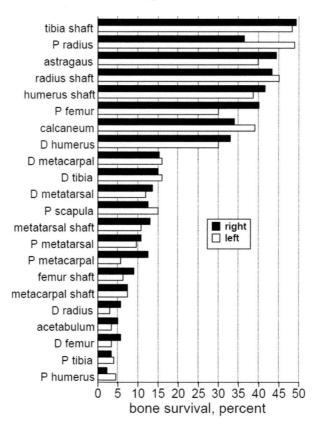

Figure 28. Pokrovnik: bone survival of caprines (P = proximal end, D = distal end).

The mammalian species found at
Pokrovnik and Danilo

Domestic species

Pig, Sus scrofa

Fragments of two pig mandibles, two maxillae and 13 post-cranial bones were identified at Pokrovnik, though all but one of these came from the later, Danilo, phase. The pig was a little more common at Danilo, with fragments of five mandibles and two maxillae, though most were found as loose teeth. Twenty-one post-cranial bones represented all parts of the body. Although the bones were few, and fewer still could be measured, some probably came from wild pigs. One metatarsal fragment from the Danilo phase at Pokrovnik was notably large, while a second from the Impressed Ware phase had a Bd measurement of 18.5 mm. Both were probably from wild pigs. At Danilo, a terminal phalanx with a length (GL) of 37.0 and a lower left M3 with a length of 36.6 mm may both be from wild pigs. The remaining pig bones were not notably large and it is very probable that these came from domestic pigs. Like the deer species, wild pigs are mammals that use closed environments for much of their feeding and resting, though capable of using open environments when food is available there. However, this is a short-term aspect of their behavior, and most foraging is done in woodland or wetland conditions. The few pig bones indicate that the environment was not favorable to this species, wild or domestic.

Sheep, Ovis musimon, and goat, Capra aegagrus

As shown above, caprines predominated at both sites, and in all levels. The caprine bones were divided into those of sheep and goat where possible, using the familiar criteria. Certain bones, notably the proximal radius, distal humerus and metapodials, were well preserved at both sites and offered reliable distinction to species in these early domestic animals. Sheep and goat were certainly present at both sites, though of the bones identified to species nearly all came from sheep. At Pokrovnik, sheep bones amounted to nearly 96% of those identified and at Danilo, 92%.

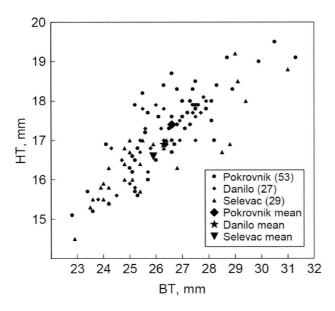

Figure 29. Pokrovnik and Danilo: measurement of sheep distal humerus compared with Selevac.

Unsurprisingly, the sheep bones from both sites indicate populations of very similar body size. The sheep humeri were compared with those from a broadly contemporary site, though from a very different environmental zone, that of Selevac in Serbia.[96] These data are shown in Figure 29, which uses the measurements BT and HT of the distal humerus.[97] The mean dimensions on the X and Y axes are also shown for each of the three sites, and these differ by less than 1.0 mm on each measurement.

The system of husbandry can best be interpreted from the age profile of the population, derived from tooth development in the mandibles. Unfortunately, at both sites these tend to be fragmented and in consequence there are many loose teeth. Even so, given that the site was carefully sieved and the recovery of even isolated teeth was good, it is possible to reconstruct the pattern of human predation on the domestic flock. The fourth lower deciduous premolar (dp4) and the permanent lower third molar (M3) are both present in the jaw for a short time. As the M3 erupts so too does the P4, displacing the dp4. With due allowance for this period of overlap, it is possible to place these teeth into the system of age classes devised by Payne,[98] though with less accuracy than is possible with more complete mandibles. There is a further limitation in that, while the dp4 can quite readily be separated into those of sheep and goat, this distinction is less reliable with the M3, possibly allowing the incorporation of some specimens from goats into the counts of older animals. The specimens were aged by the tooth eruption data given by Payne (*supra* n.[98]) and Simonds.[99]

[96] Legge 1990.
[97] Driesch 1976: Figure 32d, 76. The HT measurement is at right angles to BT as shown, on the medial margin of the condyle.
[98] Payne 1973, 1987.
[99] Simonds 1854.

Sheep: distal humerus

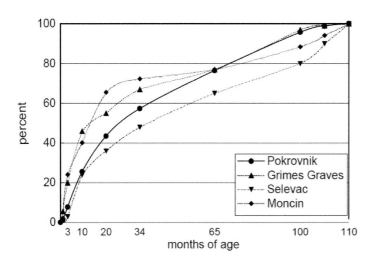

Figure 30. Slaughter patterns of sheep from Pokrovnik and Danilo compared with other sites.

While this part of the analysis is of a preliminary kind (Figure 30), the initial result shows a pattern of husbandry similar to that from the site of Selevac,[100] a site that also has excellent bone preservation with good survival of the mandibles, and was excavated with good recovery methods. About a quarter of the sheep were dead by the age of one year, rising to around 50% by two years of age. Mortality then proceeded at 6-7% for each increasing year of age. This pattern is typical of a husbandry system in which the flock provided a good deal of meat from animals killed in the 1-2 year age class. A higher rate of infantile slaughter is indicative of a more intensive extraction of energy in the form of dairy products, as is shown by data from Moncín in Spain,[101] a site also located in a semi-arid Mediterranean zone. Greenfield[102] has examined the patterns of slaughter for caprines from 15 Neolithic and Bronze Age sites in southeastern Europe, arguing that these were exploited for the 'primary' product of meat rather than the 'secondary' product of milk. Greenfield's slaughter patterns[103] show broadly similar exploitation at Neolithic sites, though both Pokrovnik and Danilo have a much higher proportion of animals killed at less than 6 months of age. At Greenfield's Neolithic sites, such infantile caprines hardly exceed 5-7% of those killed, while at Pokrovnik and Danilo this proportion is about 20%. The faunal evidence thus suggests that it is probable that a component of milk use was part of the pattern of exploitation among the caprines from the earliest Neolithic in Dalmatia. This is confirmed by the residue analysis of pottery already discussed.

However, it is possible that the difference is a reflection of the very different environmental settings of the sites, or of different modes of bone recovery. Pokrovnik and Danilo are in the Mediterranean zone while most of Greenfield's samples are from inland sites, in more continental settings, as is Selevac (Figure 30). Yet this site too has a high proportion of

[100] Legge 1990.
[101] Harrison et al. 1994.
[102] Greenfield 2005.
[103] Greenfield 2005: Figures 7, 26.

infantile mortality. Selevac had both excellent bone preservation and good bone recovery, suggesting that the difference between the inland and coastal sites arises from the bone retrieval methods employed at each. At Pokrovnik and Danilo many of the infantile and juvenile caprine mandibles were represented by isolated teeth. Only very good conditions of preservation and careful data retrieval through both dry and wet sieving will allow for the recovery of these specimens.

Cattle, Bos taurus

Cattle were not numerous at either Pokrovnik or Danilo, comprising less than 13% of the identified mandibles and less than 17% of the identified bones. However, it is probable that cattle and caprines were of about equal importance in terms of biomass, the one species being of so much larger body size than the other. In terms of body weight, food consumption and outputs sheep are commonly assessed as 7 to 10 being equivalent to one cow. There is limited evidence that some of the cattle were killed at relatively immature ages, though few neonatal bones and jaws were found that are characteristic of a highly specialized dairy economy.[104] The cattle mandible fragments and loose teeth were aged according to a system proposed by Legge.[105] This gave the following results (Table 17):

Taking the minimum number of animals that can be represented by the specimens tabulated below, at Pokrovnik there were four infantile cattle (<6 months), three juvenile cattle (15-26 months), three sub-adult (26-36 months), and three fully adult cattle (>36 months). At Danilo, there was one infantile specimen (<6 months), one young adult, and five fully adult cattle (> 36 months). Pokrovnik shows the largest proportion of young cattle, where three of thirteen specimens were killed (or died) at less than six months of age. This is an ineffective age for the best meat production, and is possibly indicative of some dairy usage of the herd. However, in the light of the small sample, it is not possible to interpret this further.

Table 17. Ages of cattle from Pokrovnik and Danilo.

Pokrovnik: cattle mandibles and teeth					Danilo: cattle mandibles and teeth				
N	Side	dp_4 wear stage	M_3 wear stage	suggested age	N	Side	dp_4 wear stage	M_3 wear stage	suggested age
1	L	2		1-3 months	1	L	3		3-6 months
3	L	3		3-6 months	1	R		6	26-36 months
3	L		5	15-26 months	1	L		6	26-36 months
1	R		6	26-36 months	3	R		7	3-6 years
3	L		6	26-36 months	1	L		7	3-6 years
3	R		7	3-6 years	2	R		8-9	6-8+ years
3	L		7	3-6 years	2	L		8-9	6-8+ years

---

[104] Legge 1990, 2005.
[105] Legge 1990.

The cattle at both Pokrovnik and Danilo were large, as is typical of Neolithic sites in Europe, though bone measurements of the rather sparse cattle bones show that at both sites they were significantly smaller than the wild *Bos primigenius* (Figure 31). The bone measurements are compared to those from Selevac, where the interpretation was that both the domestic and wild species were well represented. Figure 31 shows the measurements falling into four groups, here interpreted as being the two sexes of both domestic cattle and of *Bos primigenius*. While certain specimens are ambiguous, especially in the separation of domestic males from *Bos primigenius* females, it is evident that the few specimens from Pokrovnik and Danilo all fall within the size of a fully domestic population. Although the numbers are few, all of the measured cattle bones conform to this size and among the bone fragments there were none that showed the bone thickness and bulk that is associated with wild cattle. Local or regional domestication is therefore improbable. Further, recent studies of ancient DNA suggest that the origin of domestic cattle lay outside Europe. Analyses of a DNA extracted from cattle bones from archaeological sites widely spread though western and central Europe show that domestic cattle, both ancient and modern, have the DNA characteristic of Anatolian *Bos primigenius*,[106] though other work has indicated that there was some later crossing with wild males.[107]

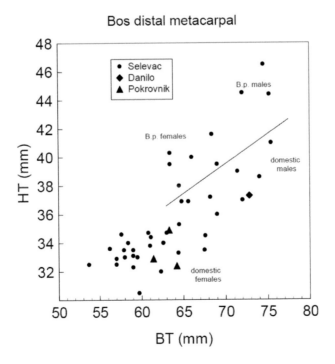

Figure 31. Distal metacarpal, cattle. Specimens from Pokrovnik and Danilo compared with Selevac.

---

[106] Anderung 2006; Beja-Pereira *et al.* 2006; Bollongino *et al.* 2005; Kühn *et al.* 2005.
[107] Götherström *et al.* 2005.

The wild species

Roe deer, Capreolus capreolus

This is a small species of deer, characteristically associated with rather dense woodland, and preferring low cover. While it is capable of adapting to more open environments, numbers are few under such conditions. The species was found to be scarce at both sites. While the fragmented bones of roe deer are of similar size and form to those of caprines, there are significant differences in morphology in both the diaphyses and epiphyses. The teeth are easily recognized, being rather low-crowned and having a characteristic fine corrugation to the enamel surface. Consequently, there is no doubt that the species was rare at both sites. Two-part mandibles, both right side and adult, were found at Pokrovnik, but none at Danilo. A single proximal metatarsal was identified at Pokrovnik; no post-cranial bones of the species were found at Danilo. These few specimens are from individuals of modest size.

Red deer, Cervus elaphus

This too is predominately a woodland deer, though capable of adapting to more open conditions when demanded, as in Scotland now. However, this open habitat is marginal for red deer and numbers are maintained through a lack of competing species and controlled human predation. The red deer is uncommon at both Neolithic sites. At Pokrovnik, a single maxillary molar was identified to this species, and no teeth from Danilo. Post-cranial bones are more common. At Pokrovnik, 17 bones were identified. These include upper limb bones (humerus, femur) and distal limb bones (astragalus, navicular-cuboid, phalanges). A curious association was found in one feature of the Danilo phase at Pokrovnik, where three right hand navicular-cuboid bones of red deer were found together. These bones have no particular utility either as implements or as toys, so that this find remains unexplained. At Danilo, no bones of red deer were identified. It might be anticipated that the identifications of red deer were from the earliest (Impressed Ware) levels at Pokrovnik, but this was not so. Six bones were identified from the Impressed Ware levels and eight from the Danilo culture levels. Three specimens are from an intermediate level between these.

The hare, Lepus capensis

Bones of the brown hare were comparatively common at both Pokrovnik (36 bones) and Danilo (24 bones). This small species would have been of minor importance in the food economy, but its presence among the wild mammal bones is notable. The hare is a species that inhabits open ground, and in the Mediterranean vegetation zone it evidently flourishes in areas made open by a degree of grazing pressure.[108] While famously fleet of foot, the hare is not an especially difficult quarry for the hunter. Although it can outrun all but the most specialized dogs, its habit of resting in a hollow scraped in the ground (a 'form') makes it vulnerable to a thrown missile when startled, or even to being grasped by a skilled stalker.[109] The few measurements that could be taken from the hares indicate that

---

[108] Karmiris and Nastis 2006.
[109] Legge and Rowley-Conwy 2000: 88.

they were of large body size for this species, conforming to those from northern Europe rather than Southwest Asia (Table 18).

The large body size of the hares from Pokrovnik and Danilo shows that the environmental conditions were satisfactory for the species, this being one of open ground rather than woodland.

Table 18. Measurements of hare bones (mm)

Bone	Modern	Pokrovnik	Syria (Mesol./Neol.)
distal humerus, Bd	12.0 (England)	12.2	10.35 (mean of 30)
	12.0 (England)	11.7	
	12.5 (England)	13.1	
	9.24 (Syria)	13.0	
Calcaneum, GL	33.6 (England)	35.5	28.5 (mean of 10)
	34.8 (England)	31.9	
	31.8 (England)		
	26.8 (Syria)		

The fauna of Pokrovnik and Danilo: environmental and economic considerations

Farming spread through Europe by the introduction of alien arable crops from Southwest Asia, these providing the calorie staple in the diet. This was supplemented by the use of foods from domestic animals, of which the sheep and goat too were alien to Dalmatia, both being species of southwestern Asia. On the other hand, wild cattle and pig were part of the indigenous fauna throughout the Mediterranean area, thus offering potential for regional domestication. The presence of sheep, goat, wheat and barley is generally accepted as the result of dispersal from Southwest Asia via the southern Balkan Peninsula. The nature of that dispersal remains the subject of some contention. Some argue that there is significant evidence that agriculture was adopted by the indigenous population, even going so far as to contend that evidence for this can be found in the presence of sheep in pre-Neolithic levels, presumably a domestic dispersal from neighboring farmers. Wild cattle and pigs would have been locally encountered, even if the species were far from common.[110] This study gives little support for these interpretations. The evidence from ancient DNA argues that domestic cattle and pigs had an origin outside Southeast Europe. While the earliest Impressed Ware levels at Pokrovnik have few measurable cattle bones, these conform wholly to the measurements of a domestic population, with no evidence for *Bos primigenius* among them. The very low proportion of wild mammals (see Figures 26 and 27 above) argues for the abrupt replacement of a natural ecology by an artificial one. A similar pattern has been found elsewhere in the Balkan Peninsula, where sites within the Mediterranean vegetation zone show a sudden appearance of domestic livestock in the earlier Neolithic period.[111]

The absence of wild cattle and the scarcity of red deer, roe deer and wild pig at both sites provide a marked contrast with the faunal sequence from the site of Selevac, a broadly contemporary settlement near Belgrade.[112] The continental climate at Selevac is very different from that found in Dalmatia, where mild wet winters and hot dry summers support typical Mediterranean vegetation. Inland, the climate has cold winters and year-round rainfall with deciduous woodland vegetation. At Selevac the arrival of Neolithic

---

[110] Miracle 2006; Forenbaher and Miracle 2005, 2006.
[111] Halstead 2006.
[112] Legge 1990

farmers was associated with a slow decline in the wild fauna, with red deer, roe deer, wild cattle and wild pig present as a major part of the fauna in the earlier levels at the site. The gradual decline of the two deer species can be followed through seven phases of the occupation.

While the nature of the vegetation in Dalmatia at 8,000 cal BP remains open to interpretation, there is good evidence that the Mediterranean vegetation zone was vulnerable to catastrophic modification, while the inland deciduous woodland was not. In Dalmatia the early farmers had the potential to bring about a rapid change to the landscape, leading to a wholly deleterious effect on the local wild fauna. In Italy there is evidence of major landscape change though the use of fire,[113] marked by the sudden emergence of more open habitat species and charcoal deposition in lake sediments. It is probable that a change of similar magnitude, possibly by the use of fire and grazing mammals, would have made an equally rapid and profound change in the Dalmatian littoral. The archaeological evidence suggests that Mesolithic settlement there was sparse, presumably reflecting the dispersed food resources of the Mediterranean climatic zone and an unproductive sea. Rather than the arrival of agriculture by a process of local domestication or even acculturation, a rapid ingress of a farming population, coupled with an absorption or replacement of the indigenous population, is better supported by this new evidence.[114]

---

[113] Colombaroli, Marchetto, and Tinner 2007; Colombaroli, Vannière, Emmanuel, and Tinner 2008.
[114] Legge and Moore 2011: 192; Moore 2015.

Marine shells

Materials, methods and results

The taxonomical analysis of the shells was carried out using the criteria of Tebble, Nordsieck and Parenzan.[115] The systematic overview of bivalve taxa and index of scientific names presented here follows the catalogue by Sabelli and colleagues,[116] while the index of common names is according to Vinja.[117] A total of 16,635 complete shells belonging to 10 bivalve taxa (Table 19) and 9,464 shell fragments belonging to 15 bivalve taxa (Table 20) were collected in the excavations. These have been identified and are presented here.

The dominant bivalve found in the samples, with a total of 16,566 shells or 99.59%, was the lagoon cockle (*Cerastoderma glaucum* [*Cardium*]). The remaining nine species were represented by only 69 specimens or 0.41%: oyster

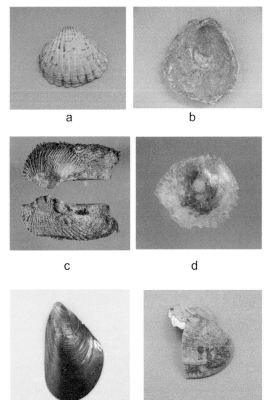

a   b

c   d

e   f

Figure 32. a, Lagoon cockle (*Cerastoderma glaucum* Poiret, 1789 [Cardium]) with hole; b, Oyster (*Ostrea edulis* Linnaeus, 1758); c, Noah's ark (*Arca noae* Linnaeus, 1758); d, Saddle oyster (*Anomia ephippium* Linnaeus, 1758); e, Mussel (*Mytilus galloprovincialis* Lamarck, 1819); f, Chequered carpet shell (*Tapes decussatus* Linnaeus, 1758). (Photo: D. Marguš.)

---

[115] Tebble 1966; Nordseick 1969; Parenzan 1974.
[116] Sabelli *et al.* 1990.
[117] Vinja 1986.

a   b

c   d

e   f

(*Ostrea edulis*) with 29 shells, Noah's ark (*Arca noae*) with 23 shells, *Chama gryphoides* with 6 shells, *Pseudochama gryphina* with 5 shells, saddle oyster (*Anomia ephippium*) with 2 shells, and the mussel (*Mytilus galloprovincialis*), chequered carpet shell (*Tapes decussatus*), European thorny oyster (*Spondylus gaederopus*) and hairy ark (*Barbatia barbata*) each with one shell (Figures 32, 33). Among the

Figure 33. a, European thorny oyster (*Spondylus gaederopus* Linnaeus, 1758); b, Hairy ark (*Barbatia barbata* Linnaeus, 1758); c, *Lutraria angustior* Philippi, 1844; d, Fragile tellin (*Gastrana fragilis* Linnaeus, 1758); e, Variegated scallop (*Chlamys varia* Linnaeus, 1758); Warty venus (*Venus verrucosa* Linnaeus, 1758). (Photo: D. Marguš.)

total of 16,566 shells of the lagoon cockle collected, 307 (1.85%) were punctured. Among the remaining bivalves, only a few Noah's Ark were punctured, and one fragment of a European thorny oyster was partially processed (filed down and made smooth). In the research conducted at Danilo in 2004, a total of 22 shells of the lagoon cockle were found in fire pits with traces of soot, perhaps indicating that these had been baked.

a   b

Figure 34. a, File shell (*Lima exilis* Wood S.V. 1839); b, Smooth venus (*Callista chione* Linnaeus, 1758); c, *Laevicardium oblongum* Gmelin, 1791; d, Rayed artemis (*Dosinia exoleta*). (Photo: D. Marguš.)

c   d

Of the total number of shell fragments collected (9,464), the most dominant taxon was the mussel (4,595, or 48.55%), followed by the lagoon cockle (4,576, 48.35%), Noah's ark (121, 1.28%) and oyster (109, 1.15%). The remaining eleven taxa accounted for only 0.67% of shell fragments: carpet shell (31), European thorny oyster (18), *Lutraria angustior* and the fragile tellin (*Gastrana fragilis*) each with three, variegated scallop (*Chlamys varia*) with two, and the warty venus (*Venus verrucosa*), *Chama gryphoides*, file shell (*Lima exilis*), smooth venus (*Callista chione*), *Laevicardium oblongum* and the rayed artemis (*Dosinia exoleta*) each with one fragment (Figures 33, 34).

Table 19. Bivalve shells by taxa collected in the excavations at Danilo in 2004 and 2005, and at Pokrovnik in 2006.

Name of bivalve	Number of shells		
	Danilo 2004	Danilo 2005	Pokrovnik 2006
Lagoon Cockle (*Cerastoderma glacum*)	3,872	12,581	113
Mussel (*Mytilus galloprovincialis*)	-	-	1
Oyster (*Ostrea edulis*)	10	14	5
Noah's Ark (*Arca noae*)	13	8	2
Chequered Carpet Shell (*Tapes decussatus*)	-	1	-
Saddle Oyster (*Anomia ephippium*)	1	1	-
Pseodochama gryphina	3	2	-
Chama gryphoides	1	5	-
European Thorny Oyster (*Spondylus gaederopus*)	-	-	1
Hairy Ark (*Barbatia barbata*)	-	1	-
TOTAL – 10 taxa	3,900	12,613	122

Table 20. Finds of bivalve shell fragments by taxa collected in the excavations at Danilo in 2004 and 2005, and at Pokrovnik in 2006.

Name of bivalve	Number of shell fragments		
	Danilo 2004	Danilo 2005	Pokrovnik 2006
lagoon cockle (*Cerastoderma glacum*)	1,172	3,283	121
mussel (*Mytilus galloprovincialis*)	1,516	1,706	1,373
oyster (*Ostrea edulis*)	27	67	15
warty venus (*Venus verrucosa*)	1	-	-
fragile tellin (*Gastrana fragilis*)	3	-	-
Noah's ark (*Arca noae*)	23	71	27

Laevicardium oblongum	1	-	-
chequered carpet shell (*Tapes decussatus*)	19	7	5
Chama gryphoides	-	-	1
European thorny oyster (*Spondylus gaederopus*)	1	15	2
file shell (*Lima exilis*)	1	-	-
variegated scallop (*Chlamys varia*)	-	2	-
smooth venus (*Callista chione*)	-	1	-
Lutraria angustior	-	-	3
rayed artemis (*Dosinia exoleta*)	-	-	1
TOTAL – 15 taxa	**2,764**	**5,152**	**1,548**

Table 21. Bivalve shells and shell fragments found by taxa collected in excavations at Danilo in 2004 and 2005, and at Pokrovnik in 2006.

Name of bivalve	Danilo	Danilo	Pokrovnik
	2004	2005	2006
Lagoon Cockle (*Cerastoderma glaucum*)	+	+	+
Mussel (*Mytilus galoprovincialis*)	+	+	+
Oyster (*Ostrea edulis*)	+	+	+
Warty Venus (*Venus verrucosa*)	+		
Fragile Tellin (*Gastrana fragilis*)	+		
Noah's Ark (*Arca noae*)	+	+	+
Hairy Ark (*Barbatia barbata*)		+	
Laevicardium oblongum	+		
Chequered Carpet Shell (*Tapes decussatus*)	+	+	+
Saddle Oyster (*Anomia ephippium*)	+	+	
Pseodochama gryphina	+	+	
Chama gryphoides	+	+	+
European Thorny Oyster (*Spondylus gaederopus*)	+	+	+
File Shell (*Lima exilis*)	+		
Variegated Scallop (*Chlamys varia*)		+	
Barbatia barbata		+	
Smooth Venus (*Callista chione*)		+	
Lutrarira angustior			+
Rayed Artemis (*Dosinia exoleta*)			+
TOTAL 18 taxa	**13**	**12**	**9**

In the excavations conducted at Danilo in 2004, a total of 13 bivalve taxa were recorded, and in 2005, 12 taxa were recorded. At Pokrovnik, nine bivalve taxa were recorded, bringing the total number of taxa identified to date to 18 (Table 21). This also means that the total taxa recorded from Neolithic sites in the Šibenik-Knin County to date is 18.

Discussion

Among the bivalves collected in the archaeological research at Danilo Bitinj in 1953, 2004 and 2005, and at Pokrovnik in 2006, it can be said with certainty that a total of 18 taxa have been identified, while 6 of the taxa claimed to have been collected by Korošec are questionable (Table 22). The find of the taxa *Cardium rusticum*, which is a synonym for the tuberculate cockle (*Acanthocardia tuberculata* Linnaeus, 1758 [*Cardium*]), was most likely confused with the lagoon cockle (*Cerastoderma glaucum* Poiret, 1789) [*Cardium*]) due to its similarity. The common mussel (*Mytilus edulis*) is a bivalve of the Mediterranean Sea and is unlikely to have been found at Danilo, and is instead probably a morphological form of the blue mussel species *Mytilus galloprovincialis* that inhabits the Adriatic Sea. Finds of the remaining four bivalves that were determined only to the genus level: *Cardium* sp., *Ostrea* sp., *Arca* sp. and *Spondylus* sp., also cannot be considered reliable. It can be assumed that, due to the morphological variability of the shells, the author listed them as separate taxa.

Table 22. Bivalve taxa collected in research at Danilo in 1953, 2004 and 2005, and at Pokrovnik in 2006.

Name of bivalve	Korošec	Marguš	Marguš	Marguš
	Danilo	Danilo	Danilo	Pokrovnik
	1953	2004	2005	2006
Cerastoderma glaucum		+	+	+
Cardium rusticum	+			
Cardium sp.	+			
Mytilus galoprovincialis		+	+	+
Mytilus edulis	+			
Ostrea edulis	+	+	+	+
Ostrea sp.	+			
Venus verrucosa		+		
Gastrana fragilis		+		
Arca noae	+	+	+	+
Arca sp.	+			
Barbatia barbata			+	
Laevicardium oblongum		+		
Tapes decussatus		+	+	+
Anomia ephippium		+	+	

Pseodochama gryphina		+	+	
Chama gryphoides		+	+	+
Spondylus gaederopus	+	+	+	+
Spondylus sp.	+			
Lima exilis		+		
Chlamys varia			+	
Barbatia barbata			+	
Callista chione			+	
Lutraria angustior				+
Dosinia exoleta				+
TOTAL	**9**	**13**	**12**	**9**

+ questionable taxa

Of the total of 18 bivalve taxa collected, 12 (lagoon cockle, blue mussel, oyster, warty venus, Noah's ark, *Laevicardium oblongum*, chequered carpet shell, European thorny oyster, hairy ark, variegated scallop, smooth venus and *Lutraria*) were collected by the residents of Danilo and Pokrovnik for food. The remaining six taxa (*Pseodochama gryphina, Chama gryphoides,* file shell, fragile tellin, saddle oyster and rayed artemis) were probably not used for food but were accidentally brought to the settlements along with the other bivalve taxa. *Pseodochama gryphina, Chama gryphoides* and the file shell were likely brought with the oyster, as they share the same habitat, while the fragile tellin and rayed artemis may have been dug up from the sand while collecting warty venus and/or chequered carpet shell. The saddle oyster was seemingly brought with the blue mussels, which it often grows on.

Conclusions

All the bivalves collected from Danilo and Pokrovnik still inhabit the Adriatic Sea today.[118] The early residents of Danilo and Pokrovnik probably collected these shells in the Adriatic near Brodarica, a 9 km walk from Danilo, or in Prukljan Lake, a brackish ria on the River Krka, 11 km from Pokrovnik and 14 km from Danilo. Of the total of 18 bivalve taxa collected, 12 were used for food, and six taxa may have been accidentally gathered during collection of edible bivalves. The small number of bivalves with traces of soot suggests that the bivalves were likely consumed raw or were boiled. The relatively small number of punctured shells of the lagoon cockle suggests that a few of these shells were used to make jewellery (necklaces, bracelets), and also perhaps for ceremonial purposes.

---

[118] Marguš 1998.

Geomorphology and soils in the vicinity of Danilo and Pokrovnik

We are reconstructing the environmental context of early agriculture in Dalmatia in order to understand local and regional resource availability during Neolithic time, and to evaluate hypotheses regarding environmental controls on site selection. Similarly, developing an archive of the magnitude and nature of early to middle Holocene environmental variation will enable us to evaluate the role environmental change may have played in the transition to agriculture.[119]

Paleoclimatic and physiographic setting

Karst landscapes in Mediterranean climates present unique challenges for environmental reconstruction, in that both landscapes and climates are spatially and temporally extremely variable.[120] Climatic archives with high temporal resolution local to the area of interest are thus needed to appropriately address questions of human ecology. Holocene records from the Adriatic region do suggest significant climatic variation during the early and middle Holocene;[121] however, it is difficult to describe regional trends given the significant local variation in records. In addition, it is extremely challenging to disentangle anthropogenic from climatic forcing of commonly used paleoenvironmental proxies (e.g., pollen, sedimentation/erosion rates). Thus, establishing a purely environmental record to be used as context for human occupation of the region remains problematic.[122]

The sites of Danilo Bitinj and Pokrovnik are located within the Dinaric karst,[123] typified by NW-SE trending ridges and (often enclosed) solution valleys or poljes. Through-going drainages within this part of Dalmatia penetrate and cut across the karst valleys, allowing for enough erosion of surficial sediments to expose middle Holocene-aged sediments at or near the surface at both Danilo and Pokrovnik.[124]

---

[119] Berger and Guilaine 2009: 429; Bonsall et al. 2002; Séfériadès 2007.
[120] Bolle 2003: 372; Calvo-Cases et al. 2003; White 1988.
[121] Andric et al. 2008; Balbo et al. 2006; Wunsam et al. 1999.
[122] Andric et al. 2008; Hanisch et al. 2003; Soligo et al. 2002; Stefani and Vincenzi 2005.
[123] Bonacci 1987; White 1988.
[124] Smith et al. 2006.

At Danilo, sediment is carried out of the polje by the Potok Dabar, an ephemeral stream that breaches the southern ridge enclosing the Danilo polje. Stream erosion within the Pokrovnik polje carries sediment to the Čikola River, a tributary to the Krka (Figure 35). Relatively steep limestone and dolomite hillslopes bounding both sites provide the potential for significant soil erosion should vegetation communities be disturbed.[125]

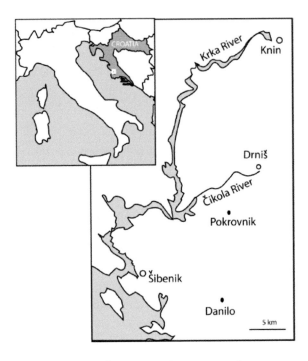

Figure 35. The Čikola and Krka Rivers in relation to Pokrovnik.

Site pedology and geomorphology

We have examined on-and offsite soils around Danilo and Pokrovnik in order to understand better the spatial heterogeneity of natural polje soil properties and thus constrain the nature of anthropogenic influence on sediments and soils observed in site excavation trenches.[126] While some differences in the chemistry and mineralogy of soils were distinguished at Danilo and Pokrovnik, soil parameters were broadly similar at both sites, suggesting similar moisture regimes and vegetation cover. Organic contents were relatively low in the soils, likely the result of millennia of agriculture. Soil thickness varied significantly (from 0 – ~2 m) in the vicinity of the sites, even though both Danilo and Pokrovnik occupy relatively low-relief surfaces. Soils within the archaeological sites were generally relatively thick (~1-

---

[125] Chen *et al.* 2009.
[126] Detailed description of site soils can be found in Fadem *et al.* 2009 and Fadem 2009; results from these works are summarized briefly here.

2 m); this thickness may reflect anthropogenic influence, or sites may have preferentially been preserved where an irregular bedrock surface allowed for deep pockets of soil to form. This was likely the case at Pokrovnik. Stable isotope analysis of soil organic matter carbon indicates C3 plant communities have dominated the region throughout the time of pedogenesis.

Soil profiles both on-and off site occasionally exhibited lenses or layers of sub-angular to angular cobbles, isolated from the bedrock by ~30–80 cm of fine-grained material. The thickness of fine-grained material between the cobble layers and bedrock suggests these coarse clasts were not derived from *in situ* bedrock weathering; however, the mode of emplacement of these cobbles remains enigmatic. It is possible that small subsurface solution cavities within the local bedrock may have collapsed, trapping fine grained cavity fill material beneath fragments of the former roof of the feature. However, such karstic collapse features are often, though not always, at a larger scale (i.e. thicker), or, when so near the surface, are composed primarily of finer-grained soil material collapsing into a void formed at the soil-bedrock interface.[127] One hypothesis involves high energy erosional events (i.e. debris flows, sheet floods) stripping material from nearby hillslopes and depositing it on flat, low-lying surfaces. Simple Revised Universal Soil Loss Equation (RUSLE)–based soil erosion modeling[128] suggests these hillslopes would have been particularly sensitive to deforestation, to a far greater degree than to changes in mean annual precipitation of the magnitude predicted for this area during the Holocene.[129] It is possible that clearance of hillslopes by or for grazing would have substantially increased regional erosion rates; however, the transport of large cobbles over distances of ~ 1km across the flat polje floor would require extremely high magnitude flooding or mass-wasting events. In addition, systems of field walls such as those present in the vicinity of the sites today would impede such long-distance transport of coarse sediments. If the cobbles observed in the Danilo soil profiles were indeed emplaced by high-energy sedimentation events, these events would most likely have occurred during a time of higher storm intensities and less vegetation cover than today, prior to any systematic construction of field walls, perhaps during the early Middle Holocene.

---

[127] Beck and Herring 2001; Parise and Gunn, 2007.
[128] Friedman 2007; Smith *et al.* 2006.
[129] Bryson and DeWall 2007.

Contemporary vegetation around Danilo and Pokrovnik

The area around Pokrovnik and Danilo is characterized by a sub-Mediterranean climate, representing a transitional type between Mediterranean and continental zones. Figure 36 plots precipitation and temperature in Šibenik and Drniš, revealing the typical overall Mediterranean pattern of precipitation concentrated in the relatively mild winter months with hot, dry summers. Precipitation at Drniš is higher and average temperatures lower than at Šibenik; however, it is the lower temperatures in the winter months that are significant and define the sub-Mediterranean zone. At Knin, for example, there are regular frosts during the winter (from December to February) with, on average, 50 days with an absolute minimum below 0⁰ C. By contrast at Šibenik there are only 17 days with similar low temperatures.[130] Inland, these lower temperatures do not allow the growth of the evergreen broad-leaved trees that can be found on the coast. In contrast, these conditions do favor deciduous trees and shrubs.

We have used the Zurich-Montpellier phytosociological method[131] in our vegetation survey. This method classifies vegetation by its floristic composition. Estimates of abundance and cover values for each species have been recorded using the extended Braun-Blanquet scale,[132] as recommended by the European Vegetation Survey Project.[133]

The climazonal vegetation of the sub-Mediterranean zone is deciduous thermophilous, and phytosociologically belongs to the order *Quercetalia pubescentis*,[134] which derives its name from *Quercus pubescens*, the downy oak (Figure 37). Two woodland associations from this order exist in the Danilo and Pokrovnik areas: mixed downy oak and oriental hornbeam, *Carpinus orientalis*, woodland (*Querco pubescentis-Carpinetum orientalis*), and European (hop-)hornbeam, *Ostrya carpinifolia*, and autumn moor grass, *Sesleria autumnalis*, woodland (*Seslerio-Ostryetum carpinifoliae*). Due to long-term human activity, the climazonal woodland vegetation of the area is heavily degraded and secondary vegetation communities, principally oriental hornbeam shrublands and extensive grasslands,

[130] Zaninović 2007.
[131] Braun-Blanquet 1964; Dierschke 1994
[132] Barkmann *et al.* 1964
[133] Rodwell *et al.* 1995
[134] Horvat *et al.* 1974.

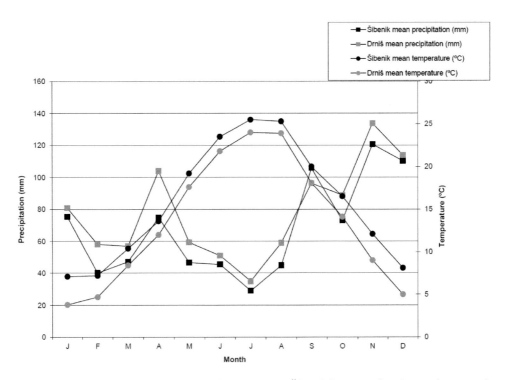

Figure 36. Mean monthly temperature and precipitation, Šibenik (1996-2005) and Drniš (1998-2005).

dominate. A commonly occurring low underbush representing degraded downy oak and oriental hornbeam woodland is characterized by the thorny shrubs buckthorn, *Rhamnus intermedia*, and Christ's thorn, *Paliurus spina-christi* (*Rhamno-Paliuretum spina christi*). Another community (*Corno-Ligustretum paliuretosum*), typical of hedges, is characterized by dogwood, *Cornus sanguinea*, and common privet, *Ligustrum vulgare*, two of the continental shrubs present in this association, mixed with Christ's thorn and other characteristically Mediterranean elements such as hackberry, *Celtis australis*.

Across extensive dry rocky areas around Danilo and Pokrovnik grassland communities predominate. On rock karst surfaces with thin soils, the most widely distributed grassland association is characterized by koeleria, *Koeleria splendens*, and Illyrian fescue, *Festuca rupicola* (*Festuco-Koelerietum splendentis*). Another association is found where even this layer of thin soil is further depleted, characterized by needle grasses, *Stipa bromoides* and *S. pulcherrim*, and common sage, *Salvia officinalis*, (*Stipo-Salvietum officinalis*). These grassland communities are maintained under conditions of high grazing intensity, wood-cutting, and occasional fires. In recent years, reduced grazing intensity and less pressure from humans have resulted in the regeneration of shrubs, most notably red-berried juniper, *Juniperus oxycedrus*, a prickly evergreen not grazed by sheep and which was formerly controlled by selective wood-cutting and occasional fires. This regeneration is viewed as a first stage in the progressive succession to oriental hornbeam underbrush and woodlands. Due to the reduction of grazing intensity in recent times, along with the highly visible widespread increase in

Figure 37. A downy oak (*Quercus pubescens*) used to stack hay.

juniper, much of the landscape today takes the form of a blend of grasslands, Christ's thorn thickets and oriental hornbeam underbrush.

On the deeper soils of the karst valleys, the poljes, more water is retained and available for vegetation, such that cultivation and mowed meadows are found there. The mowed meadows are very species rich, including endemic plants such as meadow squill, *Scilla litardierei*, and many of these species also grow in wet meadows in the continental part of Croatia. Current economic and social conditions mean that today viticulture, and to a lesser extent olives, dominate cultivated agricultural areas of the poljes (Figure 5).[135] Arable crops such as wheat and rye and their associated weedy floras are much less common than they were even in the recent past. Garden crops are still regularly cultivated in the immediate vicinity of households, along with orchard trees such as pomegranate, *Punica granatum*, fig, *Ficus carica*, and walnut, *Juglans regia*.

Two highly nitrophilous vegetation communities associated with cattle-raising and typical of the area are worthy of note. The first, which takes its name from common hard grass, *Scleropoa dura*, and greater swine cress, *Coronopus squamatus*, (*Coronopo-Scleropoetum durae*), occurs on the pathways and trails upon which cattle go daily to pasture. The second is a dwarf mallow, *Malva pusilla*, community (*Malvetum pusillae*), which develops in settlements beside byres under relatively dry, shaded conditions rich in manure. Otherwise, in settlements, along paths and around buildings, the Mediterranean ruderal community dominated by wild barley, *Hordeum leporinum*, and indicative of poor nitrophilous conditions, is common.

A dynamic landscape

This brief description of vegetation in the vicinity of Danilo and Pokrovnik highlights the sub-Mediterranean nature of the climate and vegetation as well as the overwhelming influence of human activity. Today, local people are increasingly employed in the cities and in tourism on the coast, while fewer people depend on livestock and cultivation. In

---

[135] In Figure 5 note the vine and olive cultivation in the near distance, meadows in the middle distance, and juniper overtaking formerly intensively grazed land on the north-facing far valley slope.

addition, in the first part of the 1990s, the area was part of a conflict zone that resulted in even greater depopulation of the area. Consequently, in recent decades there has been a decline in sheep and goat grazing that is encouraging regeneration of shrub and low woodlands on previously intensively grazed dry, karst grasslands. In the cultivable soils of the poljes, arable cultivation has contracted, and there has been an expansion of vine and, to a lesser extent, olive cultivation, a pattern commonly found around the European Mediterranean Basin.[136] Hay meadows continue to be maintained both in Danilo and Pokrovnik. The relatively rapid speed of vegetation alteration in the extensive grasslands highlights the responsiveness of vegetation to changes in land management practices.

In the Danilo Valley there is a marked difference between the southern and northern slopes. The microclimate of the southern slopes, which are north-facing, is somewhat cooler than the northern south-facing slopes, and the vegetation consists of denser bushes, fewer bare areas, and more deciduous species. These slopes are effectively in two different vegetation zones. This means that, as climate fluctuated in the past, there will have been considerable horizontal migration of vegetation zones across the landscape. Thus, the ecology of the region will have changed significantly with climatic variation during the Holocene in addition to the impact of human activities.

---

[136] Grove and Rackham 2003: 89.

The agricultural survey

Our research has yielded important information about the nature of the Neolithic farming economy at Pokrovnik and Danilo. To understand better the ecology of this ancient system and the key parameters within which it functioned, including climate, soils, aspect, and other factors, we decided to conduct a survey of traditional farming in the present and recent past. The need for this is urgent as such practises are changing rapidly under the pressures of large-scale economic reorientation. Thus far, we have interviewed ten local informants, including one agricultural expert, Tomislav Topić, from Drniš. The others are farmers who live in the Danilo and Pokrovnik districts.

Dalmatia, in common with the rest of Southeast Europe, has experienced a tumultuous history over the last century and a half. This has repeatedly caused significant upheavals in traditional farming, complicating our attempt to grasp its essential features and ecological foundation. Nevertheless, we have been able to identify a number of elements that have characterized farming in the region over the longer term.

The Danilo Valley, as with most poljes in Dalmatia, is parcelled into strip fields in a system that has its origins at least as far back as the Middle Ages. At Pokrovnik there are strip fields and others less regularly arranged. Individual farmers cultivate fields that are distributed across the available types, determined by soil, available moisture, and aspect. They also make extensive use of the rough ground of the valley slopes and hills for grazing. In the recent past traditional farming was for subsistence only, to feed the household. Every element of the crops grown and animals raised was consumed for food or used in other ways. The entire landscape was intensively cultivated until the twentieth century when political and economic dislocations, among them emigration to the towns and also abroad, relaxed this pressure.

The crops cultivated recently included all those raised during the Neolithic, with the exception of millet. Barley was the most common cereal grown because of its ability to withstand drought. The grains were used to make barley bread which was a local staple. Other cereals included wheat, oats, rye and maize. Among the many other crops grown regularly were peas, several varieties of beans, including fava types, chickpeas, lentils, chard, onions, and potatoes. Grass pea was cultivated for human consumption as, presumably, it was in the Neolithic. Figs were the most common fruit grown, and most farms also raised nuts, including almonds and walnuts, and a few olives. A century ago in the Šibenik region, the landscape was dominated by vineyards for the production of wine, attested today by the numerous abandoned terraces rising up the hillsides. Today cultivation of vines is once more on the increase.

Farmers cultivated small quantities of a wide array of crops to ensure that some of them, at least, would yield reasonably well despite sharp local variations in the amount and timing of rainfall from one year to another. The strategy here was based on minimizing risk through diversity. Most of the cereals were planted in the fall. They were harvested in July using sickles.

By far the most abundant animals were sheep, with some goats, followed by cattle and a very few pigs. Thus, precisely the same animals were raised, and in the same proportions, in Dalmatia recently as in the Neolithic. Lambing took place in November and December. Early winter was also the time during which animals were killed for meat. Pasture for the sheep and other animals dried up during the summer. In order to maintain their flocks, farmers would send the sheep, goats and even cattle to the mountains from June through September. A century ago transhumance was conducted on an enormous scale, with many thousands of animals making the trek each year.[137] This practise is of high antiquity, dating back to the Iron Age and beyond.[138] Our initial oxygen isotope analyses indicate that in fact at Pokrovnik it began as early as the Middle Neolithic.

One question that has puzzled us was the very low number of pigs kept on farms recently and also in the Neolithic. Farther north in Temperate Europe they would have been more common. Our informants provided the answer. In Dalmatia there is very little for pigs to eat around the farm or in the countryside during the drier summer months. Thus, a crop of wheat had to be grown especially to feed them and only a few families could afford to do this.

Predators have been a perennial problem from the Neolithic down to the present. The wolf is the chief of these. Wolves can severely deplete a flock in very short order, and would have been a source of fear and alarm from the Neolithic on. Hunted almost to extinction in Dalmatia, the wolf is now a protected species and its numbers are rising rapidly. The wolf is once again the bane of shepherds in the region who keep packs of sheepdogs to guard their flocks while they are grazing. The other main predator was the jackal, also present today, less destructive but still a hazard for smaller domestic animals.

Our preliminary conclusions from this brief review are striking. First, there is the extraordinary continuity in the farming system from the Neolithic to the present. The same species cultivated as crops then still form the basis of traditional farming today. Other crops, including several domesticated in the New World, have been added but, otherwise, the system is similar. The four domestic animals familiar from the Neolithic are characteristic of current traditional farming, and have been husbanded in similar percentages. The system then and now was designed to minimize risk in a region that experienced significant fluctuations in rainfall and temperature from one year to another. And just as farming was practised intensively until recently, we may expect that the same would have been true in the Neolithic, especially given the size of Pokrovnik and Danilo.

---

[137] Nimac 1940.
[138] Forenbaher 2011; Moore *et al.* 2007b: 32.

Commentary on results achieved thus far and their significance

Pokrovnik and Danilo together were inhabited for the entire eighth millennium and beyond, from *c.* 8,000 to 6,800 cal BP (*c.* 6,000 to 4,900 cal BC). Čista Mala – Velištak, a Hvar period site 18 km northwest of Šibenik that Podrug is excavating,[139] continues the sequence well into the seventh millennium. Thus, taken together, occupation at these three sites spanned much of the Neolithic period in Dalmatia.

The village of Pokrovnik was founded at the inception of the Impressed Ware phase *c.* 8000 cal BP and so at, or very close to, the time when farming arrived in this part of Dalmatia. The AMS dates have established this with a high degree of certainty. The Pokrovnik dates are reinforced by a similarly early date from another Impressed Ware site, Rašinovac, 21 km northwest of Pokrovnik, that is currently under investigation by McClure and Podrug.[140] Taken together, these determinations are as early as other dates for the arrival of farming and the beginning of the Neolithic in the Adriatic Basin.[141] Until recently, the prevailing model was that farming spread slowly north up the Adriatic from the south,[142] possibly in two stages.[143] We would argue on the basis of our data that there was but one spread of agriculture, and that this embraced the full mixed farming system. Furthermore, it seems to us that this new way of life expanded quickly throughout much of the southern and central Adriatic. This view is now becoming more generally accepted.[144]

The transition from the Impressed Ware to the Danilo phase at Pokrovnik, as indicated by the pottery, was a gradual process.[145] The AMS dates suggest that this took place from around 7500 to 7300 cal BP or 5500 to 5300 cal BC. Consequently, we may take the date of 5300 cal BC as the time when the Middle Neolithic became firmly established. The pottery sequences and the AMS dates indicate that pottery styles alone can no longer be used to determine cultural phases. There are too many overlaps in pottery types for this traditional

---

[139] Podrug 2010.
[140] The date is PSU-5612/UCI-AMS-127394: 7,060 ± 25 (c. 6,005-5,895 cal BP 2σ), McClure *et al.* 2014, Table 1.
[141] Forenbaher and Miracle 2005: Figure 3; Forenbaher *et al.* 2013.
[142] Skeates 2003: 171; Forenbaher and Miracle 2005.
[143] Forenbaher and Miracle 2005: 524; Forenbaher and Miracle 2014.
[144] Guiry *et al.* 2017; Kaiser and Forenbaher 2016a; Pierce 2013: 202.
[145] McClure *et al.* 2014.

approach to be sustained. Thus, *Figulina* ware, usually thought of as associated with Danilo pottery in the Middle Neolithic, first occurs as early as level 19 in Trench D at Pokrovnik, soon after the founding of the settlement. The estimated date for this early occurrence is 5700-5500 cal BC.[146] Impressed Ware in the same trench continues to be made for nearly two centuries after the earliest manufacture of Danilo pottery.

Pokrovnik and Danilo were very large villages, indeed among the most extensive of all known Neolithic settlements in the eastern Adriatic. Only some of the larger Neolithic sites across the Adriatic in the Tavoliere exceeded them in size.[147] Both Pokrovnik and Danilo had a more complex layout than we had anticipated, based on the reports of the earlier excavators. The structures we uncovered varied from trench to trench, as did the artifacts in and around them. This indicates that a range of activities was carried out across each site. We expect to provide more information on this spatial complexity as the analysis proceeds. Certainly, it will have had social as well as functional meaning. We might reasonably suppose that not all of the extensive areas covered by occupation deposits at each site were inhabited at the same time, as Korošec himself had suggested.[148] However, the AMS dates we now have from Danilo favor a second interpretation.[149] They indicate that occupation in all of the trenches was contemporaneous across the central portion of the site and thus that much of the village was inhabited at the same time. It follows that the population of Danilo, and probably of its smaller neighbor Pokrovnik, would have been large, consisting of several hundred people at least and, perhaps, significantly more at Danilo. This is likely to have been the case throughout the occupation of each site, given the stratigraphic and other evidence for continuity.

The structures in the Impressed Ware levels at Pokrovnik, the terrace walls and houses, were new in the prehistoric record for Dalmatia. This was also the case for the houses and other buildings at Danilo, a finding first manifest in Menđušić's excavations there.[150] Our exploration of the Impressed Ware phase at Pokrovnik was less extensive than the Danilo phase exposure so we cannot say much about the layout of this settlement. However, the evidence for the Danilo phase from both Pokrovnik and Danilo itself indicates that by the later eighth millennium cal BP/sixth millennium cal BC these villages were densely occupied, with structures built close together. Many of them were houses, single family dwellings in all likelihood, but there were pits excavated for building material that were later used for hearths and for depositing rubbish. Between these buildings and pits were lanes for humans and animals to pass, and open areas that may have been used to pen stock, as well as for outdoor domestic activities. It all made for a busy, packed scene of activity in every season of the year.

The artifacts, too, were novel. The pottery, above all, was a striking innovation, representing the first to be made in the Adriatic and, indeed, among the earliest to be made anywhere in the wider worlds of the Mediterranean and western Asia.[151] The Impressed ware itself was

---

[146] McClure *et al.* 2014: 1035, Figure 7.
[147] Robb 2007.
[148] Korošec 1958-1959: 148.
[149] Moore *et al.* 2007a: 21.
[150] Menđušić 1993, 1998.
[151] Barnett and Hoopes 1995; Perlès 2001. See Jordan *et al.* 2016 for a broader background discussion.

distinctive, and we need look no farther than the Adriatic for its inception. We see here the genesis of a new way of life that found expression across a wide range of artifacts used for novel purposes. These artifacts had nothing to do with the typical assemblages of the Mesolithic.

The transition from the Impressed Ware to the Danilo phase at Pokrovnik is most evident in the changes in pottery manufacture, shape and decoration. While the coarser wares remained much the same, there was a dramatic change in the finer, decorated wares. This suggests that innovations were taking place in pottery technology and style that call for further investigation and explanation. The other change of note was the appearance of obsidian; it appears that long-distance traffic in this material commenced in the Middle Neolithic. Extended maritime contacts across the Adriatic quickened and took on new aspects during this period. While we see clearly enough that these were significant developments, with probable implications for social organization, the larger meanings of these changes elude us for the moment. They will be a subject of our continued research.

The economy of the inhabitants of Pokrovnik and Danilo was based on full-time farming throughout. The crop base was broad with an array of cereals as well as legumes, among them emmer, einkorn, hulled barley, lentils, and grass pea. Other plants included free threshing wheat, millet, oats, and flax. All of these except the millet had been domesticated in western Asia long before they reached Dalmatia. The millet was probably domesticated in China.[152] The presence of numerous weed seeds reinforces this strong evidence for arable farming. Similarly, the domestic animals included all four of the main species that had been domesticated in western Asia, sheep, goats, cattle, and pigs, though in strikingly varying proportions.

While the evidence for full-time farming from the foundation of Pokrovnik at the beginning of the Impressed Ware phase is clear enough, there are indications that the system became more intensive through time. A study of sickle blades from Pokrovnik, Danilo and other sites suggests that their form and function changed in the transition from the Impressed Ware to the Danilo phase.[153] The sickle blades from the Impressed Ware phase were short, often irregular, with little retouch, and hafted in serrated fashion. Once worn out, they were replaced, a time-consuming operation. Those from the Danilo phase, in contrast, were long and regular. As the blades became worn, they were retouched in the haft, reducing the time needed to refurbish the sickle. It has been suggested that this reflects more intensive harvesting of cereals during the Middle Neolithic. This change occurred over a wide region of the central Mediterranean, including northern Italy.

Residue analysis of pottery from Pokrovnik and Danilo demonstrates clearly that the inhabitants of both sites used some vessels to cook meat, probably in the form of stews. Intriguingly, these farmers also engaged in dairying. This began in the Impressed Ware phase and became a stronger focus later on in the Danilo period. There were functional differences in usage that were closely tied to particular pottery forms. Thus, the *Figulina*

---

[152] Lu *et al.* 2009.
[153] Mazzucco *et al.* 2018.

pottery was used for raw milk. Other pottery types were used to make yoghurt and cheese, thus far the earliest documented instance of such practices anywhere in western Eurasia. Among these vessels were the rhytons, now known to have been used to hold cheese. This is the first time that it has been possible to ascribe a definite function to these otherwise enigmatic pots.

The other development in the farming system that occurred in the Danilo phase was the beginning of transhumance. Our oxygen isotope analysis has indicated that the people of Pokrovnik began to take some sheep and goats into the mountains during the summer to benefit from the better grazing to be found there. We will need to conduct further studies to establish precisely when this began and how comprehensive a shift it was, but enough has been learned already to state that this more intensive element of animal management began by the Middle Neolithic. This confirms suggestions that have already been made based on archaeological evidence that transhumance may have begun during the Neolithic in the coastal mountains of Croatia.[154] It was to remain a defining element of traditional farming in Dalmatia until the mid-twentieth century AD.

The inhabitants of both sites did very little collecting of wild foods or hunting of wild animals. Although we recovered many seashells, principally of lagoon cockles, these often occurred in batches, indicating that they were the remains of single meals for which shellfish had been boiled. Isotope analysis of pottery residues indicates that some vessels in both the Impressed Ware and Danilo phases were used to cook fish. There is nothing in the faunal remains and the artifacts, however, to suggest that fishing and shellfish harvesting provided anything more than modest supplements to the diet. The find of a single charred grape pip, interesting in itself, may indicate a precocious interest in the vine as a source of food and possibly of drink. Of course, some of the barley and wheat may also have been used to brew beer.

The evidence for transhumance carries further implications for specialization during the Neolithic. Based on recent ethnographic evidence[155] and information derived from our own agricultural survey, we can infer that only a few experienced shepherds with perhaps one or two cheesemakers will have accompanied the sheep and goats on their summer sojourn in the mountains. Similarly, it is highly likely that products such as the *Figulina* pottery were made by a few skilled craftspeople.[156] Such evidence provides clear indications of a degree of role specialization in an otherwise apparently egalitarian society.

Our evidence makes it abundantly clear that agriculture was the basis of the economy from the beginning of the Neolithic. There are no indications of an initial phase of transition: the people who established the village of Pokrovnik brought a mature, mixed farming system with them that they immediately adapted to the local landscape. Given the nature of this economy and the large size of Pokrovnik and Danilo, the agricultural activities of their inhabitants would have had a dramatic impact on the natural vegetation and soils. It is likely that the entire cultivable area within a one kilometer radius of each site was

---

[154] Forenbaher and Vujnović 2013, 20.
[155] Nimac 1940.
[156] Spataro 2009: 70.

intensively farmed. The adjacent hillsides would have offered rough grazing for stock, just as they do now. Such intensive cultivation and grazing will have degraded the vegetation and will have contributed to the loss of soil on the hillslopes and the accumulation of sediment in the valley bottoms that is so evident today.

The preliminary evidence for farming at Pokrovnik and Danilo, together with information from the agricultural survey, is sufficiently detailed for us to begin to set out the seasonal pattern of activities. The agricultural year will have begun in the autumn with the coming of the first significant rains. Once the soil was moistened, the fields would have been cleared of weeds and tilled. Presumably the tilling was done with digging sticks, wooden spades or hoes, yet there is the possibility that the inhabitants were already using ards to furrow the soil.[157] They had domestic cattle, after all, that would have served as draft animals as well as providing meat and milk. Once the land was tilled and harrowed, the main barley and wheat crops would have been sown. In September any animals taken into the mountains for summer grazing would have been brought back to the village, together with the cheeses made from their milk. This, too, was the harvest season for fruits and nuts, most of which could be dried and stored to be eaten later in the agricultural year. The need for firewood was constant as most households likely kept a fire going for cooking at all seasons. Autumn was a good time to replenish stocks from the hillslopes. As supplies of wood from nearby sources diminished, the inhabitants would have ventured farther out. Such forays would have been a weekly, even daily, occurrence during drier spells over much of the year.

The onset of the short winter season would have provided some respite from heavy labor, though the fields needed to be weeded and kept safe from intrusive grazers, domestic and wild. This was the season also for pruning fruit trees and vines. Early winter was the lambing season, itself a brief period of intense activity, and also when some animals will have been slaughtered for their meat. The quieter days of midwinter, however, may have been a time of celebration and feasting before the leaner months of late winter through early summer that followed.

Spring arrives early in Dalmatia and with it another period of intense activity. There were more fields to till in preparation for planting of the legumes, including grass pea and lentils, and also flax. Growing crops needed weeding and protection. The domestic flocks and herds could graze on fallow fields, thus helping to manure them, and also on the nearby hillslopes. Milking was a daily requirement year-round.

Once the warmer summer months arrived rainfall would have diminished, causing anxiety about the season's yields. Some animals would have been driven to the mountains in June for summer grazing. June was also the month for haymaking. This was the time to harvest and process the legumes, and then from late June through July the cereals. Once the cereals were in, the grain had to be threshed, winnowed and stored. The pace slackened towards the end of the hot summer months, allowing time for celebrations, crafts, and exchanges.

---

[157] Moore *et al.* 2000: 498.

The transition from the Impressed Ware to the Danilo phase is beginning to look more comprehensive than simply a change in pottery styles. The new forms and decoration of the pots are visually striking, but other innovations, taken together, suggest that more fundamental shifts in economy and, no doubt, other aspects of life were in train. There is the evidence for an increase in dairying, the inception of transhumance, more intensive harvesting techniques, some craft specialization, and also the traffic in obsidian with its suggestion of increased maritime contacts. These innovations took place over several centuries, apparently. While we do not understand their causes in any detail, nor their social implications, it is likely that a primary driver was growth in population as the new farming settlements became firmly established and the number of inhabitants increased. This would account for the intensification of the agricultural system.

It will be clear by now that we have succeeded in answering most of the questions we posed at the beginning of the project. The plant and animal domesticates themselves originated in western Asia and that is where this mixed farming system evolved.[158] It then spread westward, reaching Cyprus in the mid eleventh millennium[159] and Crete and the Aegean by 9,000 cal BP.[160] There followed a pause, as yet unexplained,[161] that lasted the better part of a millennium. Farming then spread rapidly from the Aegean and Greece into the Adriatic and around the western Mediterranean.[162] Everywhere, initial settlement was on the coasts and offshore islands.[163] Thus, from Cyprus to the Aegean and then to the Adriatic and beyond, it appears that the farming economy was carried forward by migrants who traveled by sea. The ancestors of these migrants came from the Aegean, and beyond from Anatolia and elsewhere in western Asia.[164] The likely stimulus for the onward migration from the Aegean to the Adriatic was the 8,200 cal BP climatic event.[165]

This disruptive episode was caused by a sudden, massive influx of fresh water from Lake Agassiz in North America into the North Atlantic.[166] This in turn led to a sharp drop in temperature and increase in aridity across much of the northern hemisphere that lasted for perhaps 300 years. Thus, while the 8,200 cal BP event was short-lived in geological terms, it extended through some 10 human generations. It would have caused severe and lengthy disruption to the simple farming systems that prevailed across the Aegean Basin and over much of western Asia. They could no longer support the densities of population that had built up through previous centuries. One solution was for farmers to move westwards and northwards in search of fresh lands to colonize. We argue that this was a powerful, primary stimulus for the movement of these migrating farmers into the Adriatic Basin.

---

[158] Zeder 2008: 11598; Moore 2014.
[159] Guilaine, Briois and Vigne 2011; Vigne *et al.* 2012.
[160] Perlès 2001: 38; Sarpaki 2009: 231.
[161] Ammerman 2010.
[162] Moore 2014.
[163] Forenbaher 2008; Forenbaher and Miracle 2005: 523; Zilhão 2003.
[164] Hofmanová *et al.* 2016; Lazaridis *et al.* 2016; Mathieson *et al.* 2018; Reich 2018: 95.
[165] Weninger *et al.* 2006; Moore 2015; Moore and Menđušić in press.
[166] Alley and Ágústsdóttir 2005.

Once these migrating farmers reached the Adriatic, they progressed northward, making full use of the offshore islands as waypoints.[167] Our evidence indicates that this movement took place swiftly. They were highly selective in their choice of places to settle, preferring valleys near the coast that offered fertile cultivable land. These migrants immediately adjusted the farming economy they brought with them to the local particularities of climate and landscape. This pattern proved to be remarkably durable, persisting in essentially the same form down to the present.

---

[167] Kaiser and Forenbaher 2016a.

References

Alley, R.B., and A.M. Ágústsdóttir 2005. The 8k event: cause and consequences of a major Holocene abrupt climate change. *Quaternary Science Reviews* 24: 1123-1149.

Ammerman, A.J. 2010. The paradox of early voyaging in the Mediterranean and the slowness of the Neolithic transition between Cyprus and Italy, in G. Vavouranakis (ed.) *Seascapes in Aegean Prehistory*: 11-29. Athens: Danish Institute of Athens.

Ammerman, A.J., and P. Biagi (eds.) 2003. *The Widening Harvest*. Boston: Archaeological Institute of America.

Anderung, C. 2006. Genetic Analysis of Bovid Remains and the Origin of Early European Cattle. Dissertation, University of Uppsala, Faculty of Science and Technology 234 (on line).

Andric, M., B. Kroflic, M.J. Toman, N. Ogrinc, T. Dolenec, M. Dobnikar, and B. Cermelj 2008. Late quaternary vegetation and hydrological change at Ljubljansko barje (Slovenia). *Palaeogeography, Palaeoclimatology, Palaeoecology* 270: 150-165.

Balbo, A.L., M. Andric, J. Rubinic, A. Moscariello, and P.T. Miracle 2006. Palaeoenvironmental and archaeological implications of a sediment core from Polje Cepic, Istria, Croatia. *Geologia Croatica* 59: 109-124.

Barkmann, J.J., H. Doing, and S. Segal 1964. Kritische Bemerkungen und Vorschläge zur quantitativen Vegetationsanalyse. *Acta Botanica Neerlandica* 13: 394-419.

Barnett, W.K. 2000. Cardial pottery and the agricultural transition in Mediterranean Europe, in T.D. Price (ed.) *Europe's First Farmers*: 93-116. Cambridge: Cambridge University Press.

Barnett, W.K., and J.W. Hoopes (eds.) 1995. *The Emergence of Pottery*. Washington, D.C.: Smithsonian Institution Press.

Bass, B. 2008. Early Neolithic communities in southern Dalmatia: farming seafarers or seafaring farmers? *European Journal of Archaeology* 11: 245-265.

Batović, S. 1966. *Stariji neolit u Dalmaciji*. Zadar: Arheološki muzej Zadar.

Batović, S. 1968. *Nin*. Zadar: Arheološki muzej u Zadru.

Batović, S. 1979. Jadranska zona, in *Praistorija jugoslavenskih zemalja II. Neolitsko doba*: 473-634. Sarajevo.

Beck, B.F., and J.G. Herring 2001. *Geotechnical and Environmental Applications of Karst Geology and Hydrology*. Lisse, The Netherlands: A.A. Balkema.

Beja-Pereira, A., D. Caramelli, C. Lalueza-Fox, C. Vernesi, N. Ferrand, A. Casoli, F. Goyache, L.J. Royo, S. Conti, M. Lari, A. Martini, L. Ouragh, A. Magid, A. Atash, A. Zsolnai, P. Boscato, C. Triantaphylidis, K. Ploumi, K. Sineo, F. Mallegni, P. Taberlet, G. Erhardt, L. Sampietro,

J. Bertranpetit, G. Barbujani, G. Luikart, and G. Bertorelle 2006. The origin of European cattle: evidence from modern and ancient DNA. *Proceedings of the National Academy of Sciences* 103(21): 8113-8118.

Bellwood, P. 2005. *First Farmers*. Oxford: Blackwell.

Berger, J.-F., and Guilaine, J. 2009. The 8200 cal BP abrupt environmental change and the Neolithic transition: a Mediterranean perspective. *Quaternary International* 200: 31-49.

Biagi, P., and M. Spataro 1999-2000. Plotting the evidence: some aspects of the radiocarbon chronology of the Mesolithic-Neolithic transition in the Mediterranean Basin. *Atti della Società per la Preistoria e Protostoria della Regione Friuli-Venezia Giulia* 12: 15-54.

Bocquet-Appel, J.-P. 2011. The agricultural demographic transition during and after the agriculture inventions. *Current Anthropology* 52(S4): S497–S510.

Bogaard, A., J. Bending, and G. Jones 2007. Archaeobotanical evidence for plant husbandry and use, in A. Whittle (ed.) *The Early Neolithic on the Great Hungarian Plain: Investigations of the Körös Culture Site of Ecsegfalva 23, County Békés*: 421-445. Budapest: Archaeological Institute of the Hungarian Academy of Sciences.

Bolle, H.-J. 2003. *Mediterranean Climate: Variability and Trends*. New York: Springer.

Bollongino, R., C.J. Edward, K.W. Alt, J. Burger, and D.G. Bradley 2005. Early history of European domestic cattle as revealed by ancient DNA. *Biology Letters of the Royal Society* 2: 155-59.

Bonacci, O. 1987. *Karst Hydrology with Special Reference to The Dinaric Karst*. New York: Springer-Verlag.

Bonsall, C., M.G. Macklin, R.W. Payton, and A. Boroneant 2002. Climate, floods and river gods: environmental change and the Meso–Neolithic transition in southeast Europe, in *Before Farming: the archaeology and anthropology of hunter-gatherers* 3-4 (2): 1-15.

Borojević, K., S. Forenbaher, T. Kaiser, and F. Berna 2008. Plant use at Grapčeva Cave and the Eastern Adriatic Neolithic. *Journal of Field Archaeology* 33: 279-303.

Braun-Blanquet, J. 1964. *Pflanzensoziologie*. Grundzüge der Vegetationskunde 3. Berlin-Vienna, New York: Springer.

Bronk Ramsey, C. 2009. Bayesian Analysis of Radiocarbon Dates. *Radiocarbon* 51: 337-360.

Bryson, R.A., and K.M. DeWall 2007. *A Paleoclimatology Workbook: High Resolution, Site-Specific, Macrophysical Climate Modeling*. Hot Springs: The Mammoth Site.

Brusić, Z. 1979. Pokrovnik, Drniš - naselje impresso i danilske faze neolitika. *Arheološki pregled* 21: 19-20.

Brusić, Z. 1994-1995. Naselje iz starijeg neolitika na Vrbici kod Bribira. *Diadora* 16-17: 1-49.

Brusić, Z. 2008. *Pokrovnik - naselje iz neolitika*. Šibenik: Muzej grada Šibenika.

Burger, J., M. Kirchner, B. Bramanti, W. Haak, and M.G. Thomas 2007. Absence of the lactase-persistence-associated allele in Early Neolithic Europeans. *Proceedings of the National Academy of Sciences* 104(10): 3736–3741.

Calvo-Cases, A., C. Boix-Fayos, and A.C. Imeson 2003. Runoff generation, sediment movement and soil water behaviour on calcareous (limestone) slopes of some Mediterranean environments in southeast Spain. *Geomorphology* 50: 269-291.

Čečuk, B., and D. Radić 2005. *Vela Spila*. Centar za kulturu Vela Luka. Zagreb: Intergrafika.

Chapman, J., R. Shiel, and Š. Batović 1996. *The Changing Face of Dalmatia*. London: Leicester University Press.

Chen, X., Z. Zhang, X. Chen, and P. Shi 2009. The impact of land use and land cover changes on soil moisture and hydraulic conductivity along the karst hillslopes of southwest China. *Environmental Earth Sciences* 59 (4): 811-820.

Childe, V.G. 1957. *The Dawn of European Civilization.* 6th ed. London: Routledge and Kegan Paul.

Colledge, S., and J. Conolly 2007a. Introduction: key themes in interregional approaches to the study of early crops and farming, in S. Colledge and J. Conolly (eds.) *The Origins and Spread of Domestic Plants in Southwest Asia and Europe*: xi-xv. Walnut Creek: Left Coast Press.

Colledge, S., and J. Conolly 2007b. The neolithisation of the Balkans: a review of the archaeobotanical evidence, in P. Biagi and M. Spataro (eds.) *A Short Walk through the Balkans: the First Farmers of the Carpathian Basin and its Adjacent Regions*: 25-38. Quaderno 12, Atti della Società per la Preistoria e Protostoria della Regione Friuli Venezia Giulia. Trieste.

Colledge, S, and J. Conolly 2007c. *The Origins and Spread of Domestic Plants in Southwest Asia and Europe.* Walnut Creek: Left Coast Press.

Colombaroli, D., A. Marchetto, and W. Tinner 2007. Long-term interactions between Mediterranean climate, vegetation and fire regime at Lago di Massaciucoli (Tuscany, Italy). *Journal of Ecology* 95: 755-770.

Colombaroli, D., B. Vannière, C. Emmanuel, and W. Tinner 2008. Fire-vegetation interactions during the Mesolithic-Neolithic transition at Lago dell'Accesa, Tuscany, Italy. *The Holocene* 18 (5): 679-692.

Conolly, J., S. Colledge, and S. Shennan 2008. Founder effect, drift, and adaptive change in domestic crop use in early neolithic Europe. *Journal of Archaeological Science* 35 (10): 2797-2804.

Costantini, L., and M. Stancanelli. 1994. La preistoria agricola dell'Italia centro meridionale: il contributo dell indagini archeobotaniche. *Origini, Preistoria e Protostoria dell Civiltà Antiche* 17:149-244.

Cummings, V., P. Jordan, and M. Zvelebil (eds.) 2014. *The Oxford Handbook of the Archaeology and Anthropology of Hunter-Gatherers.* Oxford: Oxford University Press.

Davidson, D., V. Gaffney, P. Miracle, and J. Safaer (eds.) 2017. *Croatia at the Crossroads: A Consideration of Archaeological and Historical Connectivity.* Oxford: Archaeopress.

Dennell, R.W. 1972. The interpretation of plant remains: Bulgaria, in E. S. Higgs (ed.) *Papers in Economic Prehistory*: 149-159. Cambridge: Cambridge University Press.

Dierschke, H. 1994. *Pflanzensoziologie.* Stuttgart: Ulmer Verlag.

Donahue, R.E. 1992. Desperately seeking Ceres: a critical examination of current models for the transition to agriculture in Mediterranean Europe, in A.B. Gebauer and T.D. Price (eds.) *Transitions to Agriculture in Prehistory*: 73-80. Monographs in World Archaeology 4. Madison: Prehistory Press.

Driesch, Angela von den. 1976. *A Guide to the Measurement of Animal Bones from Archaeological Sites.* Peabody Museum Bulletin 1. Cambridge: Harvard University.

Evershed, R.P., S. Payne, A.G. Sherratt, *et al.* 2008. Earliest date for milk use in the Near East and Southeastern Europe linked to cattle herding. *Nature* 455(7212): 528.

Fadem, C.M. 2009. *Geoarchaeology of the Danilo Bitinj and Pokrovnik Sites, Dalmatia, Croatia.* Ph.D. dissertation, Washington University in St. Louis.

Fadem, C.M., J.R. Smith, A. Moore, and M. Menđušić 2009. Pedologic analysis of the Danilo Bitinj site, central Dalmatia, Croatia. *Catena* 78: 181-184.

Forenbaher, S. 1999. The earliest islanders of the eastern Adriatic. *Collegium Antropologicum* 23 (2): 521-530.

Forenbaher, S. 2008. Archaeological record of the Adriatic offshore islands as an indicator of long-distance interaction in prehistory. *European Journal of Archaeology* 11, 2-3: 223-244.

Forenbaher, S. (ed.) 2009. *A Connecting Sea: Maritime Interactions in Adriatic Prehistory.* (British Archaeological Reports International Series 2037.) Oxford: Archaeopress.

Forenbaher, S. 2011. Shepherds of a coastal range: the archaeological potential of the Velebit Mountain range (Eastern Adriatic), in M. van Leusen, G. Pizziolo, and L. Sarti (eds.) *Hidden Landscapes of Mediterranean Europe* (British Archaeological Reports International Series 2320): 113-121. Oxford: Archaeopress.

Forenbaher, S. 2018. *Special Places, Interesting Times. The Island of Palagruža and Transitional Periods in Adriatic Prehistory.* Oxford: Archaeopress.

Forenbaher, S., and T. Kaiser 2005. Palagruža and the spread of farming in the Adriatic. *Opuscula Archaeologica* 29: 7-23.

Forenbaher, S., T. Kaiser, and P.T. Miracle 2013. Dating the East Adriatic Neolithic. *European Journal of Archaeology* 16(4): 589-609.

Forenbaher, S., and P.T, Miracle 2005. The spread of farming in the Eastern Adriatic. *Antiquity* 79: 514-528.

Forenbaher, S., and P.T. Miracle 2006. The spread of farming in the Eastern Adriatic. *Documenta Praehistorica* 33: 89-100.

Forenbaher, S., and P.T. Miracle 2014. Transition to farming in the Adriatic: a view from the eastern shore, in C. Manen, T. Perrin, and T.J. Guilaine (eds.) *La Transition Néolithique en Méditerranée*: 233-240. Arles: Editions Errance.

Forenbaher, S., and Z. Perhoč 2017. Lithic assemblages from Nakovana (Croatia): raw material procurement and reduction technology from the Early Neolithic until the end of prehistory. *Journal of Mediterranean Archaeology* 30.2: 189-211.

Forenbaher, S., and N. Vujnović 2013. Đurđeva greda and the Neolithic of Lika. *Prilozi Instituta za arheologiju u Zagrebu* 30: 5-26.

Fowler, C., J. Harding, and D. Hofman (eds.) 2015. *The Oxford Handbook of Neolithic Europe.* Oxford: Oxford University Press.

Friedman, J. 2007 *Modeling Modern Soil Erosion at Danilo Polje Using RUSLE.* Masters Dissertation, Washington University in St. Louis.

Gaffney, V, and B. Kirigin (eds.) 2006. *The Adriatic Islands Project. Volume 3. The Archaeological Heritage of Vis, Biševo, Svetac, Palagruža and Šolta.* (British Archaeological Reports International Series 1492.) Oxford Tempvs Reparatvm.

Gaffney, V., B. Kirigin, M. Petrić, and N. Vujnović 1997. *The Adriatic Islands Project: Contact, Commerce and Colonialism 6000 BC - AD 600. Vol. 1. The Archaeological Heritage of Hvar, Croatia.* (British Archaeological Reports International Series 660.) Oxford: Tempvs Reparatvm.

Gkiasta, M., T. Russell, S. Shennan, and J. Steele 2003. Neolithic transition in Europe: the radiocarbon record revisited. *Antiquity* 77: 45-62.

Götherström, A., C. Anderung, L. Hellborg, L. Elburg, C. Smith, D.G. Bradley, and H. Ellegren 2005. Cattle domestication in the Near East was followed by hybridisation with aurochs bulls in Europe. *Proceedings of the Royal Society*, Series B, 272: 2345-2350.

Greenfield, H. 2005. A reconsideration of the secondary products revolution in south-eastern Europe; on the origins and use of domestic mammals for milk, wool and traction in the central Balkans, in J. Mulville and A. Outram (eds.) *The Zooarchaeology of Fats, Oils, Milk and Dairying*: 14-31. Oxford: Oxbow.

Grove, A.T., and O. Rackham 2003. *The Nature of Mediterranean Europe: An Ecological History*. New Haven and London: Yale University Press.

Guarino, C. and R. Sciarrillo 2004. Carbonized cereal grains in a protohistoric house: results of hearth and house experiments. *Vegetation History and Archaeobotany* 13: 65-70.

Guilaine, J., F. Briois, and J.-D. Vigne 2011. *Shillourokambos. Un établissement néolithique pré-céramique à Chypre. Les fouilles du secteur 1*. Paris: Errance.

Guiry, E., I. Karavanić, R. Š. Klindžić, S. Talamo, S. Radović, and M.P. Richards 2017. Stable isotope palaeodietary and radiocarbon evidence from the Early Neolithic site of Zemunica, Dalmatia. Croatia. *European Journal of Archaeology* 20, 2: 235-256.

Haenlein, J. 2003. Ground Penetration Radar Investigation of the Danilo-Bitinj Neolithic Archaeological Site, Dalmatia, Croatia. M.Sc. dissertation, Cornell University.

Halstead, P. 2006. Sheep in the Garden; the integration of crop and livestock husbandry in early farming regimes of Greece and southern Europe, in D. Serjeantson and D. Field (eds.) *Animals in the Neolithic of Britain and Europe*: 42-55. Oxford: Oxbow.

Hanisch, S., D. Ariztegui, and W. Püttmann 2003. The biomarker record of Lake Albano, central Italy--implications for Holocene aquatic system response to environmental change. *Organic Geochemistry* 34: 1223-1235.

Hansen, J. 1991. *The Palaeoethnobotany of Franchthi Cave*. Excavations at Franchthi Cave, Greece. Fascicle 7. Bloomington: Indiana University Press.

Harris, D.R. 1996. Introduction: themes and concepts in the study of early agriculture, in D.R. Harris (ed.) *The Origins and Spread of Agriculture and Pastoralism in Eurasia*: 1-9. London: UCL Press.

Harrison, R.J., G. Moreno-López, and A.J. Legge 1994. *Moncín: un Poblado de la Edad del Bronce (Borja, Zaragoza)*. Coleccíon Arqueología No 16, Gobierno de Aragon. Zaragoza: Cometa.

Higgs, E.S., and C. Vita-Finzi 1972. Prehistoric economies: a territorial approach, in E.S. Higgs (ed.) *Papers in Economic Prehistory*: 27-36. Cambridge: Cambridge University Press.

Hofmanová, Z., S. Kreutzer, G. Hellenthal, C. Sell, Y. Diekmann, D. Díez-del-Molino, L. van Dorp, S. López, A. Kousathanas, V. Link, K. Kirsanow, L.M. Cassidy, R. Martiniano, M. Strobel, A. Scheu, K. Kotsakis, P. Halstead, S. Triantaphyllou, N. Kyparissi-Apostolika, D. Urem-Kotsou, C. Ziota, F. Adaktylou, S. Gopalan, D.M. Bobo, L. Winkelbach, J. Blöcher, M. Unterländer, C., Leuenberger, Ç. Çilingiroğlu, B. Horejs, F. Gerritsen, S.J. Shennan, D.G. Bradley, M. Currat, K.R. Veeramah, D. Wegmann, M.G. Thomas, C. Papageorgopoulou, and J. Burger 2016. Early farmers from across Europe directly descended from Neolithic Aegeans. *Proceedings of the National Academy of Sciences* 113(25): 6886-6891; published ahead of print June 6, 2016, doi:10.1073/pnas.1523951113.

Hopf, M. 1964. Untersuchung der Getreidereste im Hüttenlehm aus Danilo, in J. Korošec *Danilo in danilska kultura*: 107-108. Ljubljana: Univerza v Ljubljani.

Horvat, I., V. Glavač, and H. Ellenberg 1974. *Vegetation Südosteuropas*. Jena: Gustav Fischer Verlag.

Housley, R., and R.N.L.B. Hubbard 2000. The agriculture of prehistoric Servia, in C.A. Ridley, K.A. Wardle and C.A. Mould (eds.) *Servia I: Anglo-Hellenic Rescue Excavations 1971-73*

Directed by Katerina Rhomiopoulou and Cressida Ridley: 330-336. Supplementary Volume, British School at Athens, 32. London: British School at Athens.

Hunt, H.V., M. Vander Linden, X. Lui, G. Motuzaite-Matuzeviciute, S. Colledge, and M. Jones 2008. Millets across Eurasia: chronology and context of early records of the genera *Panicum* and *Setaria* from archaeological sites in the Old World. *Vegetation History and Archaeobotany* 17, Supplement 1: S5-S18.

Huntley, J. 1996. The plant remains, in J. Chapman, R. Shiel and Š. Batović *The Changing Face of Dalmatia*: 187-189. Leicester: Leicester University Press.

Isern, N., J. Zilhão, J. Fort, and A. J. Ammerman 2017. Modeling the role of voyaging in the coastal spread of the Early Neolithic in the West Mediterranean. *Proceedings of the National Academy of Sciences*; published ahead of print January 17, 2017: doi:10.1073/pnas.1613413114.

Jeffrey, C. 1959. Anacardiaceae, in C.C. Townsend and E. Guest eds.) *Flora of Iraq: Cornaceae to Rubiaceae*. Vol 4, pt. 1: 486-499. Baghdad: Ministry of Agriculture of the Republic of Iraq.

Jordan, P., K. Gibbs, P. Hommel, H. Piezonka, F. Silva, and J. Steele 2016. Modelling the diffusion of pottery technologies across Afro-Eurasia: emerging insights and future research. *Antiquity* 90(351): 590-603.

Kaiser, T., and S. Forenbaher 2012. Recognizing ritual in the dark: Nakovana Cave and the end of the Adriatic Iron Age, in H. Moyes (ed.) *Sacred Darkness: A Global Perspective on the Ritual Use of Caves*: 263-274. Boulder: University of Colorado Press.

Kaiser, T., and S. Forenbaher 2016a. Navigating the Neolithic Adriatic, in K.T. Lillios and M. Chazan (eds.) *Fresh Fields and Pastures New*: 145-164. Leiden: Sidestone Press.

Kaiser, T., and S. Forenbaher 2016b. Rite to memory: Neolithic depositional histories of an Adriatic cave, in G. Nash and A. Townsend (eds.) *Decoding Neolithic Atlantic and Mediterranean Island Ritual*: 138-159. Oxford: Oxbow Books.

Karg, S., and J. Müller 1990. Neolithische Getreidefunde aus Pokrovnik, Dalmatien. *Archäologisches Korrespondenzblatt* 20: 373-386.

Karmiris, I.E., and A.S. Nastis 2006. Intensity of livestock grazing in relation to habitat use by brown hares (*Lepus europaeus*). *Journal of Zoology* 272(2): 193-197.

Komšo, D. 2006. The Mesolithic in Croatia. *Opuscula Archaeologica* 30: 55-92.

Korošec, J. 1952. Nova neolitska kulturna grupa na području Dalmacije. *Vjesnik za arheologiju i historiju dalmatinsku* 54: 91-119.

Korošec, J. 1958-1959. *Neolitska naseobina u Danilu Bitinju. Rezultati istraživanja u 1953. godini*. Ljubljana: Univerza v Ljubljani.

Korošec, J. 1964. *Danilo in danilska kultura*. Ljubljana: Univerza v Ljubljani.

Korošec, J., and P. Korošec 1974. Bribir i njegova okolica u prapovijesno doba. *Diadora* 7: 5-33.

Kroll, H. 1979. Kulturpflanzen aus Dimini, in U. Körber-Grohne (ed.) *Festschrift Maria Hopf: zum Geburtstag am 14. September 1979*: 173-189. Archaeo-Physika, Bd 8. Köln: Rheinland-Verlag GMBH.

Kühn, R., C. Ludt, H. Manhart, J. Peters, E. Neumair, and O. Rottman 2005. Close genetic relationship of early Neolithic cattle from Zeigelberg (Freising, Germany) with modern breeds. *Journal of Animal Breeding Genetics* 122, Supplement 1: 36-44.

Kyparissi-Apostolika, N. 2002. The beginning of the Neolithic in Thessaly, Greece. 8th European Association of Archaeologists Annual Meeting, 24-29 September 2002, Thessaloniki, Hellas. Abstracts Book, 238.

Kyparissi-Apostolika, N. 2007. The identity of the Early Neolithic in Thessaly, Greece. 13th Annual Meeting of the European Association of Archaeologists, 18-23 September 2007, Zadar, Croatia. Abstracts Book, 226.

Lazaridis, I., D. Nadel, G. Rollefson, D.C. Merrett, N. Rohland, S. Mallick, D. Fernandes, M. Novak, B. Gamarra, K. Sirak, S. Connell, K. Stewardson, E. Harney, Q. Fu, G. Gonzalez-Fortes, E.R. Jones, S.A. Roodenberg, G. Lengyel, F. Bocquentin, B. Gasparian, J.M. Monge, M. Gregg, V. Eshed, A.-S. Mizrahi, C. Meiklejohn, F. Gerritsen, L. Bejenaru, M. Blűher, A. Campbell, G. Cavalleri, D. Comas, P. Froguel, E. Gilbert, S.M. Kerr, P. Kovacs, J. Krause, D. McGettigan, M. Merrigan, D.A. Merriwether, S. O'Reilly, M.B. Richards, O. Semino, M. Shamoon-Pour, G. Stefanescu, M. Stumvoll, A. Tőnjes, A. Torroni, J.F. Wilson, L. Yengo, N.A. Hovhannisyan, N. Patterson, R. Pinhasi, and D. Reich 2016. Genomic insights into the origin of farming in the ancient Near East. *Nature* 536: 419–424 (25 August 2016) doi:10.1038/nature19310.

Legge, A. J. 1990. Animals, environment and economy at Selevac, in R. Tringham and D. Krstic (eds.) *Selevac; a Neolithic Village in Serbia*: 215-242. Monumenta Archaeologia 15. Los Angeles: University of California, Institute of Archaeology.

Legge, A.J. 1991a. Animal remains from six sites at Down Farm, in J. Barratt, R. Bradley and M. Hall (eds.) *Papers on the Archaeology of Cranbourne Chase*: 54-100. Oxford: Oxbow Books.

Legge, A.J. 1991b. Bone Studies, in J. Barratt, R. Bradley and M. Green (eds.) *Landscape, Monuments and Society*: multiple entries; pp. 15. Cambridge: Cambridge University Press.

Legge, A.J. 1992. *Excavations at Grimes Graves, Norfolk: Animals, Environment and Economy*. London: British Museum Press.

Legge, A. J. 2005. Milk use in prehistory; the osteological evidence, in J. Mulville and A.K. Outram (eds.) *The Zooarchaeology of Fats, Oils, Milk and Dairying*: 8-13. Oxford: Oxbow.

Legge, A.J., and A.M.T. Moore 2011. Clutching at straw; the early Neolithic of Croatia and the dispersal of agriculture, in A. Hadjikoumis, E. Robinson and S. Viner (eds.) *The Dynamics of Neolithisation in Europe: Studies in Honour of Andrew Sherratt*: 176-195. Oxford: Oxbow Books.

Legge, A.J. and P. Rowley-Conwy 2000. The presence in historical times of the large vertebrates found at Abu Hureyra, in A.M.T. Moore, G.C. Hillman, and A.J. Legge *Village on the Euphrates. From Foraging to Farming at Abu Hureyra*: 85-91. New York: Oxford.

Lu, H., J. Zhang, K.-b. Liu, N. Wu, Y. Li, K. Zhou, M. Ye, T. Zhang, H. Zhang, X. Yang, L. Shen, D. Xu, and Q. Li 2009. Earliest domestication of common millet (*Panicum miliaceum*) in East Asia extended to 10,000 years ago. *Proceedings of the National Academy of Sciences* 106, 18, 7367-7372.

Marguš, D. 1998. *Školjkaši ušća rijeke Krke*. Šibenik: Nakladnik Javna ustanova Nacionalni park Krka.

Marijanović, B. 2000. *Prilozi za Prapovijest u Zaleđu Jadranske Obale*. Zadar: Filozofski Fakultet u Zadru.

Marijanović, B. 2005. *Gudnja: Višeslojno Prapovijesno Nalazište*. Dubrovnik: Dubrovački muzeji, Arheološki muzej.

Marijanović, B. 2009. *Crno Vrilo 1*. Zadar, Sveučilište u Zadru.

Marijanović, B. 2017. Pokrovnik – primjer ograđenoga neolitičkog naselja. *Prilozi Instituta za arheologiju u Zagrebu* 34: 5-44.

Martinoli, D. 2004. Food plant use, temporal changes and site seasonality at Epipalaeolithic Öküzini and Karain B caves, southwest Anatolia, Turkey. *Paléorient* 30(2): 61-80.

Mathieson, I., S. Alpasian-Roodenberg, C. Posth, A. Szécsényi-Nagy, N. Rohland, S. Mallick, I. Olalde, N. Broomandkhoshbacht, F. Candilio, O. Cheronet, D. Fernandes, M. Ferry, B. Gamarra, G. González Fortes, W. Haak, E. Harney, E. Jones, D. Keating, B. Krause-Kyora, I. Kucukkalipci, M. Michel, A. Mittnik, K. Nägele, M. Novak, J. Oppenheimer, N. Patterson, S. Pfrengle, K. Sirak, K. Stewardson, S. Vai, S. Alexandrov, K.W. Alt, R. Andreescu, D. Antonović, A. Ash, N. Atanassova, K. Bacvarov, M. B. Gusztáv, H. Bocherens, M. Bolus, A. Boroneant, Y. Boyadzhiev, A. Budnik, J. Burmaz, S. Chohadzhiev, N.J. Conard, R. Cottiaux, M. Čuka, C. Cupillard, D.G. Drucker, N. Elenski, M. Francken, B. Galabova, G. Ganetsovski, B. Gély, T. Hajdu, V. Handzhyiska, K. Harvati, T. Higham, S. Iliev, I. Janković, I. Karavanić, D.J. Kennett, D. Komšo, A. Kozak, D. Labuda, M. Lari, C. Lazar, M. Leppek, K. Leshtakov, D. Lo Vetro, D. Los, I. Lozanov, M. Malina, F. Martini, K. McSweeney, H. Meller, M. Menđušić, P. Mirea, V. Moiseyev, V. Petrova, T.D. Price, A. Simalcsik, L. Sineo, M. Šlaus, V. Slavchev, P. Stanev, A. Starović, T. Szeniczey, S. Talamo, M. Teschler-Nicola, C. Thevenet, I. Valchev, F. Valentin, S. Vasilyev, F. Veljanovska, S. Venelinova, E. Veselovskaya, B. Viola, C. Virag, J. Zaninović, S. Zäuner, P.W. Stockhammer, G. Catalano, R. Krauß, D. Caramelli, G. Zariņa, B. Gaydarska, M. Lillie, A.G. Nikitin, I. Potekhina, A. Papathanasiou, D. Borić, C. Bonsall, J. Krause, R. Pinhasi, and D. Reich 2018. The genomic history of southeastern Europe. *Nature* 555: 197-203 (8 March 2018) doi:10.1038/nature25778.

Mazzucco, N., D. Guilbeau, S. Kačar, E. Podrug, S. Forenbaher, D. Radić, and A.M.T. Moore 2018. The time is ripe for a change. The evolution of harvesting technologies in Central Dalmatia during the Neolithic period (6th millennium cal BC). *Journal of Anthropological Archaeology* 51: 88-103.

McClure, S.B., E. Podrug, A.M.T. Moore, B.J. Culleton, and D.J. Kennett 2014. AMS 14C chronology and ceramic sequences of early farmers in the Eastern Adriatic. *Radiocarbon* 56 (3): 1019-1038.

McClure, S.B., C. Magill, E. Podrug, A.M.T. Moore, M. Menđušić, T.K. Harper, B.J. Culleton, D.J. Kennett, K.H. Freeman, 2018. Fatty Acid Specific d13C Values reveal earliest Mediterranean cheese production 7,200 years ago. *PLOS ONE* 13(9): e0202807. https://doi.org/10.1371/journal.pone.0202807.

Menđušić, M. 1993. Danilo Gornje - zaštitno istraživanje. *Obavijesti Hrvatskog arheološkog društva* 25(2): 22-25.

Menđušić, M. 1995. Drniška krajina u pretpovijesti, in *Povijest Drniške krajine*: 9-44. Split.

Menđušić, M. 1998. Neolitička naselja na šibensko-drniškom području. *Isdanja Hrvatskog arheološkog društva* 19: 47-62.

Menđušić, M. 2005. Pretpovijesna arheološka topografija prostora župa Konjevrate i Mirlović Zagora, in *Konjevrate i Mirlović Zagora – župe Šibenske biskupije: zbornik radova Znanstvenog skupa Sela šibenskog zaleđa župa Konjevrate i Mirlović Zagora u prošlosti,* 14-16 studenoga 2002: 85-101. Zagreb.

Menđušić, M., and A. Moore 2013. The Early Farming in Dalmatia Project: an example of a successful international archaeological collaboration. *Obavijesti Hrvatski arheološkog društva* 45: 25-37.

Miracle, P.T. 2006. Neolithic shepherds and their herds in the Northern Adriatic basin, in D. Serjeantson and D. Field (eds.) *Animals in the Neolithic of Britain and Europe*: 63-94. Oxford: Oxbow.

Miracle, P., and S. Forenbaher (eds.) 2006. *Prehistoric Herders of Northern Istria. The Archaeology of Pupićina Cave.* Monografije i katalozi Arheološki muzej Istre 14. Pula: Arheološki muzej Istre.

Moore, A.M.T. 2014. Post-Glacial transformations among hunter-gatherer societies in the Mediterranean and Western Asia, in V. Cummings, P. Jordan and M. Zvelebil (eds.) *The Oxford Handbook of the Archaeology and Anthropology of Hunter-Gatherers*: 456-478. Oxford: Oxford University Press.

Moore, A.M.T. 2015. The spread of farming to the Adriatic: new insights from Dalmatia, in A. J. Ammerman and T. Davis (eds.) the Wenner-Gren Workshop on Island Archaeology and the Origins of Seafaring in the Eastern Mediterranean. *Eurasian Prehistory* 11 (1-2): 155-164.

Moore, A.M.T., G.C. Hillman, and A.J. Legge 2000. *Village on the Euphrates. From Foraging to Farming at Abu Hureyra.* New York: Oxford University Press.

Moore, A.M.T., and M. Menđušić 2004. The development of farming in the Adriatic Basin: new research at Danilo in Dalmatia. *Obavijesti Hrvatskog arheološkog društva* 36(1): 33-34.

Moore, A.M.T., and M. Menđušić in press. The first farming economy in the Adriatic: its sudden arrival and subsequent development. *Obavijesti Hrvatskog arheološkog društva.*

Moore, A.M.T., M. Menđušić, J. Smith, and E. Podrug 2007a. Project 'Early Farming in Dalmatia': Danilo Bitinj 2004-2005. *Vjesnik Arheološkog muzeja u Zagrebu*, 40(3): 15-24.

Moore, A.M.T., M. Menđušić, J. Smith, J. Zaninović, and E. Podrug 2007b. Project 'Early Farming in Dalmatia': Pokrovnik 2006. *Vjesnik Arheološkog muzeja u Zagrebu*, 40(3): 25-34.

Müller, J. 1994. *Das Ostadriatische Frühneolithikum: Die Impresso-Kultur und Die Neolithisierung des Adriaraumes.* Berlin: Volker Spiess.

Nimac, Fra F. 1940. Čobanovanje. Život i tradicije pastira dalmatinske zagore na bosanskim planinama. *Etnografska istraživanja i građa.* Knjiga II: 102-130. Zagreb.

Nordsieck, F. 1969. *Die Europäischen Meeresmuscheln (Bivalvia), vom Eismeer bis Kapverden, Mittelmeer und Schwarzes Meer.* Stuttgart: Gustav Fischer Verlag.

Novak, G. 1955. *Prethistorijski Hvar. Grapčeva spilja.* Zagreb: Academia Scientiarum et Artium Jugoslavica.

Pals, J.-P., and A. Voorrips 1979. Seeds, Fruits and Charcoals from two Prehistoric Sites in Northern Italy, in U. Körber-Grohne (ed.) *Festschrift Maria Hopf: zum Geburtstag am 14. September 1979*: 217-235. Archaeo-Physika, Bd 8. Köln: Rheinland-Verlag GMBH.

Parenzan, P. 1974. *Carta d'Identità delle Conchiglie del Mediterraneo.* Vol. 2. *Bivalvi, Prima Parte.* Taranto: Bios Taras.

Parise, M., and J. Gunn 2007. *Natural and Anthropogenic Hazards in Karst Areas: Recognition, Analysis and Mitigation.* Geological Society of London Special Publication 279. Bath: Geological Society of London.

Payne, S. 1973. Kill-off patterns in sheep and goats. *Anatolian Studies* 23: 281-303.

Payne, S. 1987. Reference codes for the wear states of mandibular teeth of sheep and goats. *Journal of Archaeological Science* 14: 609-614.

Perhoč, Z. 2009. Sources of chert in Middle Dalmatia: supplying raw material to prehistoric lithic industries, in S. Forenbaher (ed.) *A Connecting Sea: Maritime Interaction in Adriatic Prehistory* (British Archaeological Reports International Series 2037): 25-45. Oxford: Archaeopress.

Perlès, C. 2001. *The Early Neolithic in Greece.* Cambridge: Cambridge University Press.

Pierce, M. 2013. *Rethinking the North Italian Neolithic*. Accordia Specialist Studies on Italy 17. London: Accordia Research Institute.

Price, T.D. (ed.) 2000. *Europe's First Farmers*. Cambridge: Cambridge University Press.

Podrug, E. 2010. Čista Mala-Velištak: prve tri istraživačke kampanje na nalazištu hvarske culture. *Diadora* 24: 7-25.

Price, T.D. 2003. The arrival of agriculture in Europe as seen from the north, in A.J. Ammerman and P. Biagi (eds.) *The Widening Harvest*: 273-294. Boston: Archaeological Institute of America.

Rainsford. C., T. O'Connor, and P.T. Miracle 2014. Fishing in the Adriatic at the Mesolithic-Neolithic transition: evidence from Vela Spila, Croatia. *Environmental Archaeology* 19: 211-320.

Reed, K. 2006. Early Farming in Dalmatia: Preliminary Archaeobotanical Report on the Middle Neolithic site of Danilo. M.Sc. dissertation, Institute of Archaeology, UCL.

Reich. D. 2018. *Who We Are and How We Got Here*. New York: Pantheon Books.

Reimer P.J., M.G.L. Baillie, E. Bard, A. Bayliss, J.W. Beck, P.J. Blackwell, C. Bronk Ramsey, C.E. Buck, H. Cheng, R.L. Edwards, M. Friedrich, P.M. Grootes, T.P. Guilderson, H. Haflidason, I. Hajdas, C. Hatte, T.J. Heaton, D.L. Hoffman, A,G. Hogg, K.A. Hughen, K.F. Kaiser, B. Kromer, S.W. Manning, M. Niu, R.W. Reimer, D.A. Richards, E.M. Scott, J.R. Southon, R.A. Staff, C.S.M. Turney, J. van der Plicht 2013. IntCal13 and Marine13 Radiocarbon Age Calibration Curves, 0–50,000 years cal BP. *Radiocarbon* 55: 1869-1887.

Renfrew, J. 1979. The first Farmers in South East Europe, in U. Körber-Grohne (ed.) *Festschrift Maria Hopf: zum Geburtstag am 14. September 1979*: 243-265. Archaeo-Physika, Bd 8. Köln: Rheinland-Verlag GMBH.

Renfrew, J. 1989. Carbonized grain and seeds, in M. Gimbutas (ed.) *Achilleion: a Neolithic Settlement in Thessaly, Greece, 6400-5600 BC*: 307-310. Monumenta Archaeologica, 14. Los Angeles: Institute of Archaeology, University of California, Los Angeles.

Robb, J. 2007. *The Early Mediterranean Village: Agency, Material Culture, and Social Change in Neolithic Italy*. Cambridge: Cambridge University Press.

Rodwell, J.S., S. Pignatti, L. Mucina, and J.H.J. Schaminée 1995. European vegetation survey: update on progress. *Journal of Vegetation Science* 6 (5): 759-762.

Rottoli, M. 1999. I resti vegetali di Sammardenchia-Cûeis (Udine), insediamento del Neolitico antico, in A. Ferrari and A. Pessina (eds.) *Sammardenchia-Cûeis: Contributi per la Conoscenza di Una Comunita del Primo Neolitico*: 307-326. Edizioni del Museo Friulano di Storia Naturale, publicazione no. 41. Udine: Comune di Udine.

Rottoli, M., and A. Pessina 2007. Neolithic agriculture in Italy: an update of archaeobotanical data with particular emphasis on northern settlements, in S. Colledge and J. Conolly (eds) *The Origins and Spread of Domestic Plants in Southwest Asia and Europe*: 141-153. Walnut Creek: Left Coast Press.

Rowley-Conwy, P., D. Serjeantson, and P. Halstead 2017. *Economic Zooarchaeology*. Oxford: Oxbow.

Sabelli, B., R. Giannuzi-Savelli, and D. Bedulli 1990. *Catalogo Annotato dei Molluschi Marini del Mediterraneo*. Vol. 1. Bologna: Libreria Naturalistica.

Sarpaki, A. 2009 Knossos, Crete: invaders, sea goers, or previously invisible, the Neolithic plant economy appears fully-fledged in 9,000 BP, in A.S. Fairbairn and E. Weiss (eds.) *From Foragers to Farmers*: 220-234. Oxford: Oxbow.

Serjeantson, D. 2006. Food or feast at Neolithic Runnymede, in D. Serjeantson and D. Field (eds.) *Animals in the Neolithic of Britain and Europe*: 113-134. Oxford: Oxbow.

Séfériadès, M.L. 2002. Some reflections on the Mesolithic substratum and the neolithization processes in the Aegean, Danubian and Black Sea areas. 8th European Association of Archaeologists Annual Meeting, 24-29 September 2002, Thessaloniki, Hellas. Abstracts Book, 240.

Séfériadès, M. 2007. Complexity of the processes of Neolithization: tradition and modernity of the Aegean world at the dawn of the Holocene period (11-9 kyr). *Quaternary International* 167-168: 177-185.

Simonds, J.B. 1854. *The Age of the Ox, the Sheep and the Pig.* London: W.S. Orr.

Skeates, R. 2003. Radiocarbon dating and interpretations of the Mesolithic-Neolithic transition in Italy, in A.J. Ammerman and P. Biagi (eds.) *The Widening Harvest*: 157-187. Boston: Archaeological Institute of America.

Smith, J.R., R. Giegengack, and A.M. Moore 2006. Landscape and climate evolution during the Holocene in Dalmatia (Croatia): implications for early farming. 71st Annual Meeting, Society for American Archaeology, Puerto Rico. Abstracts.

Soligo, M., P. Tuccimei, R. Barberi, M.C. Delitala, E. Miccadei, and A. Taddeucci 2002. U/Th dating of freshwater travertine from Middle Velino Valley (Central Italy): paleoclimatic and geological implications. *Palaeogeography, Palaeoclimatology, Palaeoecology* 184: 147-161.

Šoštarić, R. 2005. The development of postglacial vegetation in coastal Croatia. *Acta botanica Croatica* 64: 383-390.

Spataro, M. 2009. The first specialised potters of the Adriatic region, in S. Forenbaher (ed.) *A Connecting Sea: Maritime Interaction in Adriatic Prehistory* (British Archaeological Reports International Series 2037): 59-72. Oxford: Archaeopress.

Spiteri, C.D., R.E. Gillis, M. Roffet-Salque, *et al.* 2016. Regional asynchronicity in dairy production and processing in early farming communities of the Northern Mediterranean. *Proceedings of the National Academy of Sciences* 113(48): 13594-13599.

Stančič, Z., Vujnović, N., Kirigin, B., Čače, S., Podobnikar, T., and J. Burmaz 1999. *The Adriatic Islands Project*. Vol. 2. *The Archaeological Heritage of the Island of Brač, Croatia.* (British Archaeological Reports International Series 803). Oxford: Tempvs Reparatvm.

Stefani, M., and S. Vincenzi 2005. The interplay of eustasy, climate and human activity in the late Quaternary depositional evolution and sedimentary architecture of the Po Delta system. *Marine Geology* 222-223: 19-48.

Tebble, N. 1966. *British Bivalve Seashells. A Handbook for Identification.* London: The British Museum (Natural History).

Teoh, M., S.B. McClure, and E. Podrug 2014. Macroscopic, petrographic and XRD analysis of Middle Neolithic *figulina* pottery from central Dalmatia. *Journal of Archaeological Science* 50: 350-358.

Tykot, R. 2011. Selective use of obsidian subsources on Mediterranean islands. *Abstracts*, 112th Annual Meeting, Archaeological Institute of America: 115.

Vigne, J.-D., F. Briois, A. Zazzo, G. Willcox, T. Cucchi, S. Thiébault, I. Carrère, Y. Franel, R. Touquet, C. Martin, C. Moreau, C. Comby, and J. Guilaine 2012. First wave of cultivators spread to Cyprus at least 10,600 y ago. *Proceedings of the National Academy of Sciences* 109(22): 8445-8449.

Vinja, V. 1986. *Jadranska Fauna - Etimologija I Struktura Naziva.* Vol. 2. Split.

Violich, F. 1998. *The Bridge to Dalmatia*. Baltimore: The Johns Hopkins University Press.

Weninger, B., E. Alram-Stern, E. Bauer, L. Clare, U. Danzeglocke, O. Jöris, C. Kubatzki, G. Rollefson, H. Todorova, and T. van Andel 2006. Climate forcing due to the 8200 cal yr BP event observed at Early Neolithic sites in the eastern Mediterranean. *Quaternary Research* 66: 401-420.

White, W.B. 1988. *Geomorphology and Hydrology of Karst Terrains*. Oxford: Oxford University Press.

Whittle, A. 1996. *Europe in the Neolithic*. Cambridge: Cambridge University Press.

Wunsam, S., R. Schmidt, and J. Mueller 1999. Holocene lake development of two Dalmatian lagoons (Malo and Veliko Jezero, Isle of Mljet) in respect to changes in Adriatic sea level and climate. *Palaeogeography, Palaeoclimatology, Palaeoecology* 146: 251-281.

Zaninović, K. 2007. Klima i bioklima Nacionalnog parka 'Krka', in D. Marguš (ed.) *Simpozij rijeka Krka i Nacionalni park Krka prirodna i kulturna baština i održivi razvitak*: 67-78. Šibenik: Javna ustanova Nacionalni park Krka.

Zeder, M.A. 2008. Domestication and early agriculture in the Mediterranean Basin: origins, diffusion, and impact. *Proceedings of the National Academy of Sciences* 105(33): 11597-11604.

Zilhão, J. 2003. The Neolithic transition in Portugal and the role of demic diffusion in the spread of agriculture across West Mediterranean Europe, in A.J. Ammerman and P. Biagi (eds.) *The Widening Harvest*: 207-223. Boston: Archaeological Institute of America.

Zohary, D. and M. Hopf 2000. *Domestication of Plants in the Old World: The Origin and Spread of Cultivated Plants in West Asia, Europe and the Nile Valley*. 3rd ed. Oxford: Oxford University Press.

Zvelebil, M., and M. Lillie 2000. Transition to agriculture in eastern Europe, in T.D. Price (ed.) *Europe's First Farmers*: 57-92. Cambridge: Cambridge University Press.